Autobiography of a Geisha

AUTOBIOGRAPHY OF
a Geisha

Sayo Masuda

Translated by G. G. Rowley

Columbia University Press   New York

792.7
M42a

Columbia University Press
Publishers Since 1893
New York   Chichester, West Sussex

Geisha: Kutō no hanshōgai by Sayo Masuda
Copyright © 1957 by Sayo Masuda
Original Japanese edition published by Heibonsha Ltd., Publishers
English translation rights arranged with Heibonsha Ltd., Publishers
through Japan Foreign-Rights Centre.

Translation copyright © 2003 Columbia University Press

Library of Congress Cataloging-in-Publication Data
Masuda, Sayo, 1925–
   [Geisha: Kutō no hanshōgai. English]
   Autobiography of a Geisha / Sayo Masuda ; translated by
 G. G. Rowley.
     p. cm.
   Includes bibliographical references.
   ISBN 0–231–12950–5 (cloth : alk. paper)
   1. Masuda, Sayo, 1925– 2. Geishas—Biography. I. Title.

GT3412.7.M37 A3 2003
792.7'028'092—dc21
[B]

2002041020

Columbia University Press books are printed on permanent and durable
acid-free paper.
Printed in the United States of America
c 10 9 8 7 6 5 4 3 2 1

Contents

Acknowledgments

Over the years when I was working on this translation, I benefited greatly from opportunities to talk about geisha, and Masuda Sayo's memoir in particular, at several different venues. I am grateful to audiences at Amherst College, the Deutsches Institut für Japanstudien in Tokyo, Guilford College, Latrobe University, the Nissan Institute of Japanese Studies at the University of Oxford, Oxford Brookes University, the University of Sydney, the University of Alberta, and the University of North Carolina at Chapel Hill for their many valuable questions and suggestions. To the organizers of these various occasions—Patrick W. Caddeau, Nicola Liscutin, Hiroko Hirakawa, Rajyashree Pandey, Arthur Stockwin, Joy Hendry, Nerida Jarkey, Janice Brown and Sonja Arntzen, and Jan Bardsley—I am indebted for their warm and gracious hospitality.

Mr. Komiyama Kiyoshi, my neighbor in Tokyo, kindly prepared the maps; I am grateful for his technical expertise and imaginative vision. Special thanks also to Lesley Downer, Toby Eady, Joshua Mostow, and Elise Tipton for their advice and encouragement.

For taking time to read the first draft of the translation and patiently pointing out what was still unclear, I thank my parents, Kenneth and Nancy Rowley, and my sisters, Pamela Rowley and Stephanie Rowley Wood.

I am also grateful to Yokoyama Toshio of the Institute for Research in Humanities, Kyoto University, who was particularly generous in helping me with correspondence, and Haruo Shirane of Columbia University, who opened doors when I was in search of a publisher.

My readers for Columbia University Press, Liza Dalby and William Johnston, were magnanimous in their enthusiasm for the project and offered many helpful suggestions for improvement. Edward G. Seidensticker also kindly read the entire manuscript at short notice and made several important corrections.

The final stages of research were facilitated by a grant from the Waseda University Special Projects Fund. I would also like to thank Jennifer Crewe, editorial director at Columbia University Press, for her stalwart guidance throughout, and Margaret B. Yamashita and Irene Pavitt for their expert copy editing and good humor.

My greatest debt, of course, is to Thomas Harper, who found Masuda Sayo's memoir for me. His support has been unwavering and his critical acumen unfailing. This translation is for and because of him.

Autobiography of a Geisha

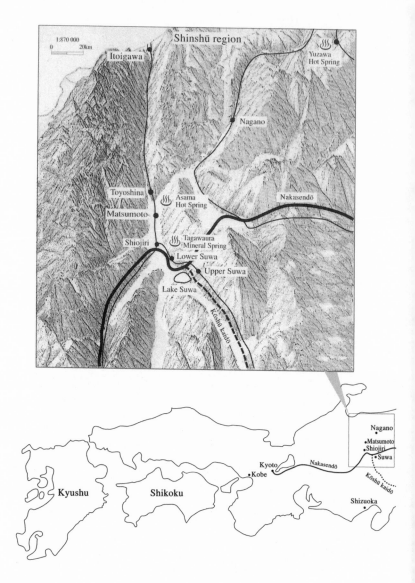

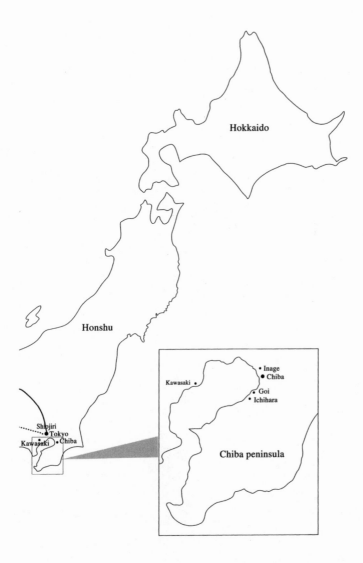

Translator's Introduction

Masuda Sayo was a geisha, and this is the story of her life. It is a life that bears little resemblance to that of the glamorous Kyoto geisha depicted in Arthur Golden's best-selling novel *Memoirs of a Geisha* or Hida Chiho's *Forty Years in Shinbashi*, the elegant geisha quarter in Tokyo frequented by politicians and industrialists. Masuda was a geisha at a hot-springs resort, where the realities of sex for sale are unembellished by the aura of rich, famous, or powerful patrons, and the arts of song and dance that are the geisha's stock in trade are often simply bawdy, even lewd. We catch brief glimpses of these lower reaches of the geisha world in Kawabata Yasunari's renowned novel *Snow Country*, but Masuda's autobiography gives us a totally unaestheticized picture of its realities, which for her amounted to "half a lifetime of pain and struggle," the subtitle of the Japanese text translated here.[1]

Masuda was born in 1925 near the town of Shiojiri in Japan's mountainous Nagano Prefecture. A measure of the region's poverty is that more people emigrated from Nagano to the Japanese puppet state of Manchukuo, established in March 1932 in northeastern China (Manchuria), than from any other prefecture in Japan.[2] Masuda's parents were not legally married, and her mother left her with an uncle, who cared for her until she was five or six years old. She never knew her father. At an age when she should have begun to attend primary school, Masuda's uncle sent her to work as a nursemaid (*komori*) for a landowning family. Her earliest memories are of this period in her life, painfully recalled in the first chapter of her autobiography.

When Masuda was about twelve, her mother, by this time married with four small children, needed money to pay for her husband's medical treatment. Masuda's uncle was sent to retrieve his niece from the landowners. The following day she was sold to a geisha house (*okiya*) in the hot-springs resort of Suwa, a former castle town on the shores of Lake Suwa in Nagano Prefecture.[3] In accordance with custom, she first served as a novice in the geisha house, working as a maid while training in the geisha arts of dance, song, shamisen, and drum. In her sixteenth year, 1940, she made her debut as a geisha. Chapters 2 and 3 of Masuda's autobiography take the story of her life up to this point.

MASUDA WROTE her autobiography in 1956/1957, more than a decade after she had left the geisha world. Very few geisha have written their memoirs. To the best of my knowledge, Masuda's is the only full-length autobiography by a former hot-springs-resort geisha in existence. Most such geisha, like the model for the character Komako in Kawabata's *Snow Country*, have preferred to disappear into obscurity.[4] Why, then, did Masuda, who had no illustrious clients she could describe, decide to write the story of her life? For one thing, she was desperately in need of money. By the mid-1950s, she was in her early thirties and living hand-to-mouth, working first in a restaurant and then as a farmhand, being paid 350 yen (a little less than a dollar) a day.[5] She seems never to have contemplated making a living teaching shamisen or dance, as some former geisha do; in any case, such artistic training as she had received was long in the past. Masuda had never attended school and was barely able to write only because a former lover had encouraged her to learn the rudiments. But attracted by prize money that the magazine *Housewife's Companion* (*Shufu no tomo*), the most popular women's magazine in 1950s Japan, was offering in its "True Stories by Women" competition, Masuda decided to attempt an account of her life. Written entirely in the *hiragana* syllabary taught to children in their first months at school, the manuscript amounted to fifty pages of ruled paper. The editors of *Housewife's Companion* awarded it second prize of 150,000 yen and published it in the February 1957 issue of the magazine under the title "Account of the Wanderings of a Country Geisha."

The editors at *Housewife's Companion* also embellished Masuda's voice, giving it an elegant polish: the language is polite; the narrator is quietly self-effacing; and the frequent use of structures from the classical language lend the text a literary refinement that could hardly have been the work of the author. Moreover, the account is utterly devoid of the humor that enlivens the later book-length version.

Masuda's short memoir was spotted by the editorial director of the Heibonsha publishing house, who decided to ask her to expand it into a book. Oda Mitsuki, the editor assigned to the task, wrote to her in the simple *hiragana* script, and three months later, a new version—three hundred pages this time—arrived at his office. So visually memorable was the manuscript that a reproduction of one page was included in the original edition; it reveals an unformed hand that might be mistaken for that of a primary-school student. Masuda's natural style, too, was "breathless . . . colloquial, immediate, delivered by a narrator who is so much part of the scene that [s]he explains nothing."[6] Obviously, some work would be needed to turn this into a publishable text. But Oda was afraid that if he corrected the manuscript himself, its power and intensity would be lost. He decided to visit her. They sat facing each other across a desk, he asking questions, she writing down the answers; he refrained from writing anything at all himself, he says. In this way he managed to preserve her voice as the editors at *Housewife's Companion* had not. The book-length version of Masuda's autobiography was published in August 1957 and, reprinted in various formats over the decades, remains in print today. My translation is based on the revised version edited by Oda and published in the Heibonsha Library series in 1995.[7]

Besides the desire to make a little money, Masuda had another important reason for writing her memoir. She was motivated, she says, by a sense of outrage at what she felt was the hypocrisy of the Prostitution Prevention Act, which had gone into effect in April 1957. Enforcement of this act effectively brought an end to licensed prostitution (*kōshō*) in Japan, a system whereby the government officially sanctioned prostitution by women, licensed for the purpose, in designated areas. The act specified that these women could now be arrested and sent to a guidance facility for "rehabilitation." But whatever the intentions of the act's supporters, its passage did not, of course, end prostitution in Japan. It succeeded only in criminalizing the entire prostitution industry and the women who, for whatever reasons, wished to continue working as prostitutes.[8]

"Just passing laws banning prostitution isn't going to accomplish anything," Masuda predicted. She knew because she had been there herself. Her memoir records that in the summer of 1952, her younger half brother, whom she had brought up on her own since leaving the geisha world, was diagnosed as suffering from tuberculosis, the largest single cause of death in Japan throughout the first half of the twentieth century. Once he was admitted to hospital, their savings from working as black-market traders were soon exhausted, and Masuda could not earn enough on her own to pay for his medical treatment. The only option she could see was to begin working as a prostitute. Masuda doesn't reveal exactly how much more she earned in this way, but there is some evidence that at least allows us to speculate. Writing in the newspaper of the Yoshiwara Women's Health-Preservation Union in 1956, union vice president and prostitute Takeo Shizuko estimated that women working in the Yoshiwara red-light district of Tokyo earned about 30,000 yen a month.[9] Masuda had worked in a smaller red-light district in Chiba City four years earlier and thus cannot have earned this much. Nonetheless, even if she earned only half as much, say 15,000 yen a month, as a prostitute, that was more than twice as much as the 6,000 yen per month she was able to earn trading on the black market. When her brother was healthy and working, they could manage and even save a little; but without his contribution and with the added burden of his medical bills, she saw no alternative but to sell her body. Masuda's plight as well as her attitude toward the Prostitution Prevention Act were typical of many Japanese women who worked as prostitutes in this period: women supporting parents whom the war had left incapable of earning a living, women from districts where the local coal mine or factory had closed down, women trying to escape the chronically low wages of female occupations such as those in the textile industry. "Among those making the laws," Masuda asked, "were there any women like us who couldn't have survived if they hadn't prostituted themselves?" There were not. And so after surviving her stint as a prostitute and returning to her native Nagano Prefecture, Masuda decided to write her autobiography.

IN CONTEMPORARY JAPAN, no young woman *has* to become a geisha. For centuries, though, being indentured to a geisha house or, worse, a brothel was something that could happen to any woman if her family fell into debt.[10] In her autobiography, Masuda uses the word *urareru*, an adversative passive form meaning "to be sold against one's will," to describe what happened to her and other young women. Technically, of course, she was not sold; the sale of human beings had been illegal in Japan for hundreds of years.[11] Rather, Masuda was indentured for a period of time unknown to her and for a sum she estimates at about 30 yen.[12] The going rate for girls indentured to geisha houses in Suwa at that time (around 1936) was between 30 and 100 yen for a ten-year indenture. Masuda assumes she would have changed hands for no more than the lower sum: she was completely illiterate and also badly sunburned from working outdoors in an era when pale complexions were prized. For Masuda's mother, however, 30 yen was a vast sum of money, as a glance at the contemporary price of rice reveals. In Tokyo in 1935, the retail price of 10 kilograms of polished (white) rice was 2 yen, 50 sen. Assuming that rice in Nagano cost about the same as in Tokyo, this means that Masuda was sold for the equivalent of about 120 kilograms of rice, almost enough to feed one adult for an entire year.[13]

But the poor could not afford to eat white rice. As Masuda herself discovered when she returned to her birthplace some years later, they ate barley and sweet potatoes and subsisted at a level of material deprivation that shocked her deeply. Pet cats at geisha houses ate better than the parents of many geisha. In chapter 6 of her memoir, Masuda gives us a rare glimpse of the grinding poverty of the rural poor in wartime Japan.[14] It was from this level of society that the majority of geisha, serving women (*shakufu*), and prostitutes (*shōgi*) were recruited.

The romanticization of geisha life as dedicated principally to the pursuit of traditional arts ignores the poverty that drove many parents to indenture their daughters to geisha houses. Such romanticization also erases certain geisha from the collective memory and overlooks the bottom line of the whole geisha business. The geisha thus erased are hot-springs-resort geisha, and the bottom line of the geisha business is, of course, sex for money. At the glamorous high end of the geisha world, in the Pontochō and Gion districts of Kyoto and Shinbashi in Tokyo, sex may seem a less obtrusive aspect of the geisha business. But at the lower end, in a hot-springs resort like Suwa where Masuda worked, sex with geisha was the expected end of every evening.

One of Masuda Sayo's aims in writing her autobiography was to describe this bottom line. In her sixteenth year, after the party at which she made her debut as a professional geisha, Masuda underwent sexual initiation (*mizuage*) at the hands of her patron (*danna*), who had paid her house handsomely for the privilege. The mother of her geisha house then sold her "virginity" four more times. Masuda's description of this is brisk and completely devoid of self-pity. In his afterword, Oda writes that he asked her whether it was really true that she didn't resist the system of sexual initiation "and so forth." Masuda explained to him that becoming a fully fledged geisha meant rising in the world and an easier life, that sexual initiation was not nearly so bad as being hungry or in pain. It was only "after she had known love" (*koi o shitte kara*), she said, that she felt some resistance to sleeping with men she didn't like.[15]

Geisha like Masuda catered to the passing trade of a hot-springs resort. It was a world in which anyone could become a customer. As Masuda explains: "Normally, when you stayed the night with your *danna*, he paid only for your time; and when you spent the night with someone who wasn't your *danna*, you received double points; and when you just slept with a customer without staying the night, it was ten points." Points thus earned were tallied up and put toward paying off the debt to her house that a geisha accumulated over the years, a debt that included the cost of her original indenture, kimono, and artistic training. In this passage and elsewhere in her memoir, Masuda demolishes the notion that geisha do not provide sexual services for payment. She makes it clear that in the world she inhabited, geisha routinely engaged in sex for payment ("points"), that this is what was expected of them, and that to pay for sex with a geisha required no special introduction or intermediary: anyone who could afford it could patronize geisha.

Because of the transient nature of the hot-springs-resort geisha's clientele, hers could never be a glamorous world. The only regular patrons in Masuda's day were local factory owners and their sons, small-time entrepreneurs, and petty gangsters. Venereal disease was a constant occupational hazard, and Masuda's memoir contains a grim description of the slow death of one of the other geisha in her house from untreated venereal disease. Pregnancy was regarded by the geisha in her world as a curse; Masuda herself was relieved when her first pregnancy ended in miscarriage, and she seems never again to have conceived.

The line between hot-springs-resort geisha and prostitute is obviously a thin one, and in her autobiography, Masuda does not elaborate on the distinction. But as we have been told by both Japanese and foreign observers for a hundred years or more, the difference between geisha and prostitutes is *gei* (art), which geisha have and prostitutes do not.[16] In Jodi Cobb's photographic account of 1990s geisha life, a geisha named Mayumi describes the difference in this way:

> In the past, a daughter would be sent to a geisha house to keep her family from debt or starvation, just as in Vietnam and Cambodia and Thailand today parents are selling their children. But there, it is mere prostitution, just the selling of bodies. There is no pride for the girls, no skills to call their own, nothing to emerge with. But in the geisha world, the saving grace is that even though you may enter with nothing, you will come out with your own skill, your world of art. That's a huge thing you gain.[17]

Mayumi is right to the extent that some geisha were (are) able to retire from the day-to-day work of entertaining and survive economically as teachers of one of the traditional arts that geisha practice.

Women's mastery of these arts also gave them good cause for personal pride, a means by which they could live at least a part of their lives following the dictates of their own desires rather than the desires of others.[18]

If Masuda found some sustenance in the arts she learned, she does not tell us about it. She recalls only the way in which they were beaten into her. But Masuda's years of experience in the art of entertaining did make her an accomplished storyteller. She has a marvelous memory for conversations and voices, which she worked consciously to develop. As a result, *Autobiography of a Geisha* is as often remarkable for its humor and wit as for its unromanticized frankness. Masuda can see the comical side of many an event that a less resilient person might have found crushing. One example is particularly telling:

> This customer didn't seem to like the coolly elegant geisha type. I'd once heard some talk of Hugo and Rodin, so I just repeated what I'd heard. He was delighted. "What an intellectual you are!" he said. As he became more and more serious about me, I could almost feel my hands closing around him. I knew I had him.

We see here not simply a finely tuned wit at work but also the extraordinary resourcefulness with which Masuda overcame the handicap of illiteracy to become a brilliant conversationalist—in a subject she knew nothing about. This same effort, applied to the subject she knows best of all—her own life—has produced a revealing and moving record of a woman's survival on the margins of Japanese society. Nor is this all, for in finding her own voice, Masuda also enables us to hear the voices of many other women less able to make themselves heard: nursemaids, apprentice geisha, gangster mistresses, the rural poor, postwar black-market traders, and prostitutes. *Autobiography of a Geisha* is at once the superbly told tale of a woman whom fortune never favored yet never defeated and a panorama of life in a little-known world which for most of its inhabitants is one of constant "pain and struggle."

Chapter 1 &~ A Little Dog, Abandoned and Terrified

My earliest memories are of being a nursemaid in the home of landowners in the rural district of Gōhara, near Shiojiri in Nagano Prefecture.[1] I remember almost nothing from my childhood, but these people must have been large landowners because they hired three farmhands on yearly contracts; and at busy times, such as the planting season, they would take on fifteen or sixteen more. The property was surrounded by a dense growth of trees, and there were a number of large chestnuts. I would be scolded severely for the least little thing and lived in constant fear of any sign of people. Yes, when I think back to my childhood, what first comes to my mind is a vision of myself tied to a chestnut tree after being scolded, bawling my eyes out. For some reason, caterpillars seem to fall off chestnut trees rather easily, so there were always great swarms of caterpillars scattered about under the trees; and then they would congregate at the roots and start crawling sluggishly up the trunk. I loathed caterpillars, but being tied up, I couldn't get away even when they were crawling all over my body. Almost faint with dizziness, I would weep. I think that must have been when I was about six years old.

At the time I wasn't even able to wonder why I didn't have any parents or why I should be the only one who was tormented. If you ask me what I did know then, it was only that hunger was painful and human beings were terrifying, that was all. How to hide so that people couldn't find me? How to fill my stomach? These were the only two thoughts in my life.

As for filling my stomach, I was entirely at the mercy of others for my meals. There was a chipped bowl that they left under the sink in the kitchen into which they put their leftover rice and soup. If there were lots of leftovers, then even with just that one bowl I'd be full; but if nothing had been left, then that was that. After everyone had finished eating, I would go to the kitchen and peer into the bowl, and if something was in it, I would quickly crouch under the sink and eat it.

My bed was a hempen sack stuffed with rags thrown into a corner of the storehouse. I would crawl into it legs first, the rags rustling as I pushed them apart, and go to sleep. But in the middle of the night I would have to pee. The storehouse is dark and scary. And so while I'm putting it off, I fall sleep again. Even if I had an accident, I didn't mind, because in the morning it would still be warm; but come evening when I put my legs in, it would be cold and damp and, "Oh no!" I would remember what happened the night before. It felt disgusting and I couldn't get to sleep at all; and so when that happened, I would look for a place outdoors in the shadows and sleep curled up like a dog.

But winter in the Shinshū region is cold, and so it wasn't easy. *Never* will I have another accident, I would think; but when night fell, in spite of myself I'd be afraid again. And so I often ended up sleeping outside. It was not only the nights that were cold. When I was minding a child, even though my back would be warm from carrying it, my feet would be as cold as ice. In winter, no matter how cold it was, I was never allowed to wear socks; and so I would lift one leg up and warm my foot on the thigh of the other leg, doing this over and over again so that I was always standing on one leg. That's how I got the nickname "Crane."

Nor was it only the adults who tormented me. If I were foolish enough to let myself be found by the children, I would always be forced to do something that I found painful. They called it "playing dog." The children would spit something out onto the ground. Then they would make me get down on all fours, bark "yap yap" and run around in circles, and then pick the thing up with my mouth. If I were to say "No!" they would do something horrible to me, stamp on my toes, pinch me, or kick me. Out of fear, I would give in. I must have made a good toy for those children.

When I first arrived there, they said I was infested with lice or something and shaved my head. I suppose it was then that the children would ask, "Hey, nurse, are you a boy or a girl?" And I would pull up my skirts and show them my bottom. In the end they found it so funny that whenever they saw me they would jeer, "Pull it up! Pull it up!" When I turned eight or nine, although no one taught me, I came to understand, by instinct I suppose, what it was to feel shame. And then if I tried to escape them, they would bar the way and tell me that if I didn't pull up my skirts, they wouldn't let me through. "Nursie, crane, monkey baby!" they would jeer, "Is your bum bright red?" When I burst into tears, they would let me go. If I cried, the children loved it. "Ha ha! Monkey baby cried!" they would shriek in delight as they scattered. I seem to have caught on and made a point of always crying in the end so I could get away.

The eyes of the oxen glow in the dark

About my work: They woke me up at about five in the morning and made me do the washing in the stream.[2] There are two kinds of streams in the countryside: streams for washing dishes and streams for washing clothes. In winter, all the streams are frozen, but at the places where everyone does their washing, the ice is thinner. You would break the ice at those thin spots and wash the diapers there. Since I was a child and did things slowly, the washed diapers would already be frozen by the time I was ready to rinse them. Blowing hard on my chapped hands, I'd soak the diapers in the water all over again and then rinse them. When the washing was finished, I'd do the cleaning, and then at last it was time for breakfast; after that the actual child minding began.

The household consisted of grandfather, grandmother, and a young married couple. My job was to look after the children of this couple. There were many servants, too, and one day the following incident occurred.

In order to test me, they said, they had left 2 sen someplace where I was likely to see it, and the money had disappeared. I hadn't so much as seen it; I didn't even know how to use money in those days, but they accused me of taking it to buy sweets, and I was scolded. They told me to kneel down and apologize with both hands on the floor. "It wasn't me!" I muttered, but that only made matters worse.

"Put her in there until she confesses!" With that I was locked in the storehouse, and they didn't let me out for two days. There were bales of unhulled rice piled up in the storehouse. By poking my fingers into them I managed to extract a bit of rice, which I chewed up, but for two days I didn't have a single drop of water to drink. It was so painful I thought I was going to die. Even so, it never occurred to me to protest in a loud voice that I didn't know anything about anyone taking any money, so why were they doing such cruel things to me? I simply endured whatever was done to me and lived in constant fear.

When I think back on it, it's just possible that 2 sen really did disappear. But with no evidence they couldn't very well accuse an adult of stealing it, so most likely they bullied me as a warning to the other servants.

In the summer there were more melons in the field than anyone could eat, and they would rot. Now I never got even a decent mouthful of melon pickle, so I would sneak into the field, squat down, and eat some of the melon on the sly. I was careful not to let anyone see me, but somehow they always found me out.

"You've been in the melon field again, haven't you?" they'd say, slapping me three or four times on the cheek.

"I'll never go there again!" I'd apologize; and I'd really mean it, but when I got hungry, off I'd go again. And be found out straightaway. Finally they said, "The next time you do that we'll throw you in with the oxen!"

The ox stable is scary. They would throw me in there in the middle of the night, which would spook the oxen and upset them. I'd be kicked and butted something dreadful. Their eyes, glowing in the dark, are terrifying; even now I just can't help being frightened of oxen. So again I vow never to go near the melon field. And again, without really meaning to, there I'd go. Again, I'm found out, immediately. I'm terrified of the ox shed; and no matter how much they accuse me, I insist that I never go to the melon field.

"So you never go there? Then what's this?" they say, thrusting a child's diaper under my nose.

So that's why I was always found out! The riddle was solved. When I was squatting down in the melon field, chewing away, the child on my back was stuffing whatever it could reach into its mouth. And the melon leaves emerged in its stool.

After that, it was decided that such a creature as I could never be trusted to look after their precious children. I was put to work weeding the fields and, in the autumn, driving home oxcarts loaded with unhulled rice from the rice paddies. But oxen are scary and I wasn't able to make them go where I wanted them to. Once a wheel of the oxcart slipped down over the bank of a small stream. I was at my wit's end when a man who lived in the neighborhood passed by, and with great effort, he managed to pull it out for me.

"A little thing like you. . . . This is far too hard! You must be exhausted." He spoke so gently to me that I almost began to sob. Without thinking I blurted out, "Yes! It's too hard!" A few days later Grandfather called me in.

"When you can't even do your own work properly, how is it that you're complaining to outsiders about the family?" he said angrily, picking up a stake and flinging it at me. There were nails sticking out of the stake, and my hands were injured. The injury became infected and in the end it had to be treated by a doctor.

"Not only do you cause us grief, you cost us money. No more food for this troublemaker!" he bellowed. "And she's not to sleep under this roof anymore, either!" How I regretted being so careless as to trust that neighbor. I hadn't complained to him about anything, yet what a tattletale he'd been. Never trust anyone: that was the lesson that this experience engraved on my heart.

I, TOO, HAD A MOTHER

Writing as I do, it may seem that I spent every day in tears, full of sadness; but I also had quite a few secret pleasures.

At the farm there were large walnut and chestnut trees, and I used to pick up the nuts when no one was looking. I seem to have had a bit of good sense in this matter, for I hoarded them in a secret place of my very own. In winter I would stealthily take them out and eat them. Chewing on a raw, dried chestnut is deeply delicious.

The walnuts I would crack open with a stone and eat. This task gave me a great deal of comfort in my loneliness. Otherwise, I would go someplace where no one else was around and just squat down, very still, and in that way I could pass a bit of time in peace.

How many years I lived there I couldn't calculate; but one New Year's, a person they called "Uncle" came and told me that he would take me to my mother's place. I had never before been so happy as I was then. But because I was always being called "Monkey baby, Monkey baby!" without even thinking I asked, "Is my Ma a real human being?" Uncle laughed.

So even I have a mother. What sort of a person is she? Where does she live? I wanted to meet her now. I headed for the house, walking in front of Uncle. Other children have parents, and so they go to school. They get sweets. They get to wear socks. Maybe I'll get to wear socks, too.

But my mother didn't show me a single gesture of kindness; she just looked me over coldly. In a dimly lit house with sloping eaves, a man was lying down; four children surrounded me and stared at me from a distance with intense curiosity. Looking back, I now realize that among them was my poor little brother who later committed suicide.

I stayed there only one night; the next morning, again led by Uncle, I trudged on. On the road, Uncle told me for the very first time how I happened to be born. I was a fatherless child and thus a social embarrassment; and so as soon as I was born, I was taken in by Uncle, who was my mother's younger brother. It was a struggle for him to support me for those first five years, so when an acquaintance of the landowners came with the suggestion that I be given to them as a nursemaid, he handed me over. This is what Uncle told me; and when he had finished, he said, "You poor, poor child." Even now I remember the frail sound of his voice as he spoke.

It made me feel a bit the way you would if your father had done something nice for you, and I walked along merrily down the path knee-deep in snow, swinging on Uncle's hand as if something delightful were waiting at the other end.

In fact, at that very moment I was walking toward the event that would determine the rest of my life: I was to be sold as a geisha. Yet even if I had not been sold as a geisha, for someone like me, there could never be any road to happiness.

Even now it fills me with anger: I want to rage against the miserable lives we lead, those of us who are born into this world as blots of sin because of a parent's irresponsibility; I want to cry out that a life like mine must never be repeated. No matter how deep in disgrace, a human being *is* human, after all. The human spirit wanders ceaselessly in search of light; and if it finds a light of some sort, it strives somehow to get near it, struggling, writhing in anguish. Yet even as it writhes in anguish, it is drowned before it reaches the light. If you have the heart of a human being and you become the parent of a human being, then even if it exhausts every bit of your energy, until that child can walk alone I want you to do your duty as a parent.

Chapter 2 The Sunburned Novice

Unable to go to school, unable to read, I had grown up as an abandoned dog does; and then at the age of twelve, I was sold. Actually, I didn't know how old I was; but around that time I heard
someone saying that that child was twelve, and I recall thinking "So
I'm twelve years old then, am I?" Given that, it must have been
about 1936 or 1937.

The place I was sold to was a geisha house (*okiya*) in Upper
Suwa called the Takenoya. At first I was wide-eyed with astonishment at its splendor, like a palace in a dream. Uncle was talking
about something in a low voice with the master of the Takenoya,
bowing his head lower than necessary and incessantly wiping the
tip of his nose with his tightly clenched handkerchief. I crouched
down behind him, making myself as small as I could. My face was

burned black by the sun, but my eyes must have flashed with curiosity as they darted about the room.

"Looks like a river sprite, this one."

The first words to reach my ears were those of "Mother," the
mistress of the Takenoya. For some reason I felt embarrassed and
hung my head low in shame. Before long, the transaction must
somehow have been settled. Uncle said, "From now on, you'll be a
child of this house, so do as the master tells you and make yourself
liked." Then he left through the tradesman's entrance.

I was put in the bath, given a change of clothes, and taken to my
Elder Sisters' room. I was utterly amazed. Kimono and underrobes
more beautiful even than those the daughter of the landowner had
worn to festivals were hanging there on bamboo hangers. Once,
when I was a nursemaid, I'd taken a peek at one of the daughter's
picture books. There was a drawing of a beautiful palace in it, and
I'd whispered to Mii-chan, the tenant farmer, "What's this?" "It's
the Palace of the Dragon King," he told me, "and the pretty princess
is Oto Hime." Now, really, it seemed as if I'd ended up in the Palace
of the Dragon King and so my Elder Sisters must be Oto Hime.
How happy I'd be, I thought, if I, too, could live in such a beautiful place![1]

But the rigors that began the following day taught me that this
was not the soft life I'd thought it would be, that this was no haven
of refuge. Up in the morning, wipe down all the woodwork, wash
the clothes of all nine people in the house, run errands; then in the
evening, traipse after my Elder Sisters carrying their shamisen; and
when necessary—when they stayed over—fetch a change of clothes
for them. Mother and my Sisters ordered me to do one chore after
another; there wasn't a moment when I could have relaxed. And
never a word with which they didn't hurl some sort of abuse. You
fool! You idiot!

When I first arrived, Father had asked me what my name was,
and I'd replied, without a moment's hesitation, "Nursie."

"There's no such name as Nursie," he laughed.

"It's Crane," I quickly corrected myself.

"Crane? That's better."

So it was "Crane" I was called, but then they all decided they'd call me "Low," as in "low intelligence."

Still, I was happier than I'd been before. After all, I could always get sweets. When my Elder Sisters were in a good mood, they'd hide in their sleeves the bonbons and sponge cake they were given at parties and bring them back for me. At the landowner's house, I'd *seen* sweets but never had been given any.

It was about this time that I was first taken to see a "moving picture." "Oh dear," I thought, "how pitiable some people in this world are!" I cried so hard my head hurt. I went on crying for days whenever I would think about it. "Have you ever seen such a stupid fool?" my Sisters laughed; but no matter how many times they explained to me that it was only a story, only a movie, I simply couldn't swallow it. "Just as I thought—it must be because I'm not really a human child; that's why I don't understand." This was how I explained it to myself.

In the movie, there was a child who was blind and his mother who worked somewhere as a maid. The little blind boy accidentally kicked over a kettle and said, "What a hard wooden sandal!" His mother saw this and decided to kill herself; but when she went outside, she saw a hen feeding its chicks. She gave up the idea of dying. That was all; but even now, twenty years later, it's still etched into my memory.

GEISHA SCHOOL

After I'd been here about a month, I was sent to geisha school. As a rule, novices didn't go to regular school; they went to the geisha school run by the geisha registry office. Even on our way to and fro, we'd be pestered by the local bullies if they spotted us.

"Hey! Here come the geisha kids! What a stink! What a stink!"
they'd say, throwing stones at us, making faces, jeering.

There was another novice at the Takenoya who had come before
I did. She was a year older than me, and she said she'd been there
for three years, so she would have been ten when she arrived. She
was called Hamako, and she had long hair that she tied back so
tightly it pulled her eyes up at the corners; at the back, she wound
it round in a bun. Her appearance somehow gave the impression of
a delicate and fragile person. But Elder Sister Hamako was tremen-
dously brave. "Little Crane," she would say, "we're not running
away!" and then she'd give as good as she got. "Hey, moron! Brat!
Your old man stinks, too, he does!"

"Who do they think they are? Their own fathers buy geisha; and
they're completely besotted with them, I'll bet! You just watch! I'll
show them! Beasts! How I hate them!" Her cheeks would flush
with excitement as she spat out the words.

Hamako was pretty, so I suppose Mother had high hopes for her
future; at any rate, she scolded her far less frequently than me. In
those days, as soon as my hair would grow out, it would be hacked
off short, and so it was always sticking out. I looked just like a river
sprite and, to top it all, was a skinny runt besides. "When you compare Little Hamako with Little Crane, they're as different as a
princess and a foot soldier's daughter," they'd laugh. In my heart,
child though I was, I was ashamed of myself and longed to be beautiful. I'd come to believe that to be beautiful was the most important thing in the world, and the most beneficial. A beautiful girl
sold well, which meant that she could do just as she pleased and
lord it over everyone else.

At the geisha registry school, the shamisen teacher was thin and
strict and covered with freckles. In lessons we sat facing one another and learned by watching her every move. If you made two
or three mistakes, suddenly her plectrum would fly down and hit
you hard on the knee. As a novice, there was never a time when I

didn't have bruises on my knees. Nor was the plectrum of the shamisen the only pain we had to endure: at dancing lessons, the teacher's ruler would lash out and whack your hand, your leg, anywhere. I was surprised how much it hurt to be whacked with a ruler. Was this a kindness, meant to whip us into shape as quickly as possible? Or a punishment, because they despised us as things to be bought and sold? Yet if they were teaching a young lady of means, I was sure, they wouldn't treat her this way, even if she did make a mistake.[2]

At the time, if there had been a kindly god or some such who had said to me, "I won't hurt you physically or mentally, I promise, so tell me the truth. What is it you're most afraid of?" I would have answered immediately, "People." And if that god had said, "I'll grant you just one wish," I'm sure I would have answered, "I want to go somewhere there are no people."

They also taught writing at the geisha school. But no one cared much whether or not you learned your letters. Figuring I'd reduce the pain, even by one whack if I could, I threw myself totally into learning shamisen, drum, and dancing and made no attempt to learn my letters.

Shortly after I started at the geisha school, they picked the coldest time of the year to conduct "cold practice." We were seated along a verandah open to the elements and practiced shamisen and drum. At home we were put through "cold practice" by our Elder Sisters; and if I made two or three mistakes, they, too, would say, "Something stuffed up in your head, is there? Well, cool off for a while and give it some thought!" and storm off. You had to sit there, repeating the same passage over and over again with all your might, until they said, "That'll do. Stand up." The hand with which I beat the drum was so cold it ached, and blood ran from the cracks. In spite of myself, tears welled up in my eyes. For two hours or so, I could bear it; but when you're forced, brutally, to remain seated for three hours, your mind starts to go blank, and, from the cold, I suppose, it becomes impossibly difficult even to think straight. If I happened to be caught crying by one of my Elder Sisters, I was in for a terrible time.

"So this little one enjoys crying, does she? Well if you want to cry that much, then go ahead, bawl your eyes out!" they'd say and then drag me out and throw me down into the snow.

At such times, all I could think was, "Why was I ever born?" I hated my parents who had brought me into this world and then just cast me aside. The despair is more than I can put into words.

I WANT TO BE A GEISHA, RIGHT NOW

It was the first flower viewing in the geisha quarter since I'd come to Suwa. I was stunned again by the beauty. Not the beauty of the cherry blossoms but of my Elder Sisters who gathered beneath the trees in all their finery. The flower viewing was held every year in a park that was on the site of the old castle of Suwa, a domain that had been valued at 30,000 *koku*. Within the small inner moat, the castle walls rose high, built of bright, neat stones, and an air of elegance lingered in the ruins. The remains of what must have been the great keep stood still higher; from there you could gaze out over all of Upper Suwa and as far away as Lower Suwa. Beneath the cherry trees that had been planted all over the ruins, mats and rugs were spread out, and everyone enjoyed a boisterous good time, urging one another to sing and dance. All the geisha, of course, were being paid for their time, and the sight of them making the most of the day—for they had no hope of a better tomorrow—was both sad and beautiful.

"No! If Mother sees us we'll be scolded!" I protested; but Elder Sister Hamako dragged me along on our way home from lessons, and in that stolen moment we caught a glimpse of the goings on.

"Why not? I'll make my debut next year, so I've got to take a look. Don't you want to start going to parties soon, too?" Her eyes sparkled as she spoke. And I, too, though I couldn't have admitted it, felt the same longing to be a geisha. Because geisha wore pretty kimono and didn't have to do the washing, and they didn't have to run errands either.

Spring passed and summer arrived. That summer was the only time I ever looked back fondly on my days as a nursemaid at the landowner's. They say that cats know the most comfortable places to spend the summer and the winter, but I knew them, too. When I had a child on my back, I could stroll about in the shade of the trees, where there was a cool breeze. And when I was a nursemaid, I wore hardly any clothes. But now, although I was only a novice, they made me dress up properly in a cotton kimono: "because you're going to be a geisha." During dancing lessons I fairly dripped with sweat and broke out in prickly heat rash all over my body. On top of this, I was ordered to do one chore after another and had to spend the whole day running about obediently. I didn't have a spare moment to wipe away the sweat!

Mother could do perfectly beastly things, but Father was a gentle man and would often mutter to her under his breath, "There's no need to go that far." Even so, he seemed incapable of saying anything stronger than that. When Mother would say to him, "What would you know about it?" he would look glum and fall silent, pretending he hadn't noticed anything. Much later I learned that Mother, too, had once been a geisha and had got to know Father then. His family discovered that he was spending money on geisha, and he was disinherited to prevent his frittering away the family's assets. Mother was in love with him and was willing to do anything to be with him. So she seduced the master of the geisha house where she worked and then created a huge to-do about how she couldn't possibly stay in a place where the master had his hands all over her. At the end of the whole messy business, they say, she ran out on her contract. After that, she worked as a maid at an inn, and by conning men, even stooping to steal from the rooms, she got together the money to start her present business. If the story's true, then even now I think I can understand how she felt.

My four "Elder Sisters"

There were four geisha at the Takenoya.[3] Elder Sister Takechiyo wasn't particularly popular, but she'd been there the longest; she was bad tempered and domineering. If she came home drunk, she'd always wake me up in the middle of the night and send me out to buy cigarettes. You'd think that when she realized she wouldn't have enough, she'd buy some in advance, but she thought nothing of tormenting others. There was no way the tobacconist would be open at two or three in the morning. She herself ought to have known that from her own days as a novice, but if I came back and said that they weren't open, she'd scold me and say, "Stand outside until they are then!" There was nothing else to do but to go back to the shop and wait there. After a while I began to cry, and when a passing drunk stopped to ask me what the matter was, I told him. He gave me a packet in which five or six were left, and thus I learned that from now on the thing to do was to look for a drunk and cry in front of him.

Elder Sister Karuta was gentle and the kindest of all to me; she often used to give me sweets. Once I broke Mother's teacup and didn't have the courage to go and apologize because I knew I'd be scolded again. As I stood there trembling, Karuta asked me, "What's the matter?" When I indicated the broken cup and asked for her help, she said, "That's nothing to cry about!" and paying no attention to me, she boldly went and, with both hands on the floor, bowed low before Mother.

"I've been inexcusably careless," she said, pointing out the teacup.

"It is inexcusable, but if you clean it up there'll be no need to call the police," Mother said, glancing up, but she said nothing further. I think Karuta got away with it because she was popular with customers.

Elder Sister Takemi was apparently suffering from peritonitis brought on by gonorrhea. From about the time I arrived at the house, her whole body would be swollen when she woke up in the morning. She looked pale and sick, but she had a straight nose and beautiful eyes. She treated me neither badly nor kindly, but never once did she call me "Low," either. There was something a bit slow about her, and Mother was always bellowing at her; but she never gave the slightest impression of caring and always had a faint smile on her face. Not for a moment, though, could I ever think her stupid. Quite the contrary: the impression that remains with me even now is that she was the most intelligent of us all. Her stomach was all puffed up, and it hurt her to eat anything, she said. Takechiyo couldn't bear to look at her.

"Why don't you go to the doctor? You'll die, you know, if you go on like that," she warned her.

"There's nothing in this world I'd regret leaving behind. If I can die even one day sooner, that'll be one day sooner I'll be at peace. As they say, dying is paradise, living is hell. I want to go to paradise just as soon as I can," she said with a smile and not the least shadow of doubt on her face.

The bamboo, they say, blossoms and forms seed every so many years—or is it every so many hundreds of years?—and anyone who sees this is supposed to live happily ever after. How true it is I don't know, but I've heard that Takemi took her name—"Bamboo Seed"—from that legend.

Elder Sister Shizuka was so beautiful she looked as if she'd stepped straight out of an *ukiyoe* woodblock print. She gave herself airs and was quite a chatterbox. She'd seize on a story about someone and gabble on and on as if she knew everything there was to know about it. Then Takechiyo would say, "What a busybody! Why don't you just shut up!" Shizuka didn't like being told off and would reply crossly, "You've got a nerve, talking to me like that, and when you're hardly selling at all." This is the nasty sort of talk I would hear.

Shizuka loved novels and if ever she had any free time, she'd lie face down, engrossed in her reading. All her books were about the popular hero Zenigata Heiji, and all together she had twelve of them, I heard.[4] If she was in a good mood, she'd read them to me.

"What do you think? Fabulous, isn't he! If this sort of a man was around here, I wouldn't hesitate to make him mine. How I adore him! Just thinking about Heiji makes my heart throb," she said excitedly, her eyes shining. I had no idea then that novels were figments of the author's imagination, and meaning to pay her a compliment, I said very timidly, "I'd like to meet him, too. If you meet him, Sister, promise me you'll let me meet him once, too?"

"What an idiot this child is! It's just disgraceful that someone like her says she wants to become a geisha!" She derided me mercilessly, and once it got around, I became for a time the butt of everyone's jokes. Better not to say anything, I thought, quite convinced now that if I didn't understand the reason for something, it was because I was stupid.

Shizuka was moody: one moment she'd be patting you on the cheek, the next she'd slap it. And once every month, she'd cry uncontrollably. If I told one of the others, "Elder Sister Shizuka's crying," they'd only say, "Just leave her alone," and take no notice. At such times, even if she had bookings, she'd dawdle and procrastinate and eventually leave the house in tears. I was under the impression that people cried only when they were really unhappy, so one day I informed Mother that Shizuka was crying.

"She's hopeless, that one. Once a month, when nature takes its course, she has the urge to cry uncontrollably. She's got the crying disease."

Even if she did have the crying disease, it seemed to me, she couldn't be crying for nothing. "Shouldn't she be seen by a doctor then?" I carefully watched the expression on Mother's face.

"Why on earth did we take in such an idiot? You'll never amount to anything! Just go and call Shizuka!" Every ounce of contempt in her showed on Mother's face as she spoke. Shizuka, who had come at Mother's call and taken my place, seemed to be taking a terrible tongue-lashing. I bitterly repented that what I'd meant as a good turn had gone so wrong. Frightened for her, I stood stock-still and listened, careful not to make a sound.

"If you don't like it here, you're welcome to move out anytime you like! You're not cut out to be a geisha, are you? A geisha, I can tell you, even if she is a bit good looking, will never sell if she gets stuck up. You're really better suited to be a whore; so go on and be one, starting tomorrow!"

"Mother, forgive me, please! I'll work hard, and earn as much as I can!"

As I listened to her tearful entreaties, I realized I had understood nothing, that never should I have said a word without being asked; I was quite overcome with remorse. In those days, decisions about a geisha's lodgings were entirely at the whim of her proprietor; her own wishes counted for nothing. The police just stood by as human beings were openly bought and sold. Mother let Shizuka off, and the instant she came out and saw me she slapped me hard on both cheeks.

THE DEATH OF ELDER SISTER TAKEMI

In the Shinshū region, spring comes late and autumn early. By the middle of September, the mornings and evenings are chilly. Around that time Elder Sister Takemi, who'd been injecting herself constantly, saying "My stomach hurts," finally took to her bed. For a time, though, if she were wanted at a party, she'd go. Her face was flushed and shiny, probably from the fever, but her skin was covered in goose bumps.

"I used to think that a person could will herself to bear anything, but illness—there's nothing you can do about that." She was smiling as she spoke, without a trace of sadness in her expression.

Around that time, I heard that a child from another geisha house, with whom I'd often trained at the geisha school, had been killed. My Sisters talked of nothing else whenever they were together. It was pitiful, they said, for all she'd done was eat one sweet cake worth 1 sen. Her Mother had caught her eating it and, stuffing a rag into her mouth, said, "If you're so hungry then eat this!" They rolled her up in a mattress and threw her into a cupboard. Then everyone just forgot about her. By the time they remembered and dragged her out, her body was cold. How she must have suffered! She'd peed and the mattress was soaking wet, they said. They summoned her parents and gave them 100 yen, and they took her body away, bowing and scraping, so the story went.[5]

"What a terrifying world this is," one of my Sisters said, "when you can buy someone's life for 100 yen."

"No," said another, "it was bad luck that her heart stopped beating just then; she was an unlucky person."

"Just because we're bought and sold, it doesn't mean our lives are for sale."

And so it went. No one seemed to know the truth of the matter. They were saying whatever happened to pop into their minds, but the fact remained that the child was dead.

In the midst of all this, it was Takemi who said, "I really wonder whether those who die are the unlucky ones, and those who live are the lucky ones." Not long after this, even when she was wanted at a party, she wouldn't go out but spent all her time singing to herself. I thought she must be lonely, lying in bed all by herself, and so after everyone else had gone out to work, I went up to the second floor. Father, Mother, and the novices slept downstairs; the geisha's rooms were upstairs. Takemi was asleep, looking as if she had completely exhausted all her reserves of strength and spirit. Sensing me sitting there, she opened her eyes. "Is that you, Little Crane?" She smiled weakly.

"You're a good girl, you are. They all say you're useless, but that's not so. You're honest and decent, I think. I wish someone as decent as you didn't have to go into this kind of work, but it can't be helped. It's all decided by the time we're born what we're going to have to do. I've been true to my fate. Whatever's asked of you, do it faithfully and quickly; got that? If you do, you'll be able to get to paradise that much quicker. I'm a human being, too, and there were things I wanted to say, things I wanted to do, someone I liked, or half liked anyway. But I knew nothing could come of it, and so I gave up. Before long you'll come to understand too, Little Crane, so do me a favor and remember what I've just said. At long last I'm going to be at peace."

She spoke as if in a trance, or delirious with fever, and stared at me with her beautiful eyes. "Have you got that? You'll remember me, won't you? You mustn't ever forget," she insisted, over and over. "People mustn't ever do anything that causes others to carry a grudge against them. Because someday, in some other form, it'll come back to haunt them." Before long, I'd come to understand, she said over and over again, gripping my hand in her hot hands and smiling her beautiful smile.

Even now, I remember it all so clearly I can still hear her voice. Why? Because I'd never been treated with such overwhelming honesty as I was then; I'd never before been touched by such warm hands. Although I'd never hated people, never tried to scheme against them, every good turn I'd tried to do for others had ended in failure; I'd always been jeered at and tormented. Takemi wasn't despairing or sad; she had the beautiful smile that only those who see things as they really are possess. I'll never forget her as long as I live. At the time, I didn't yet understand what she meant; I simply concluded that beautiful people were beautiful even when they were sick.

Not long after this, she was at peace. By the time it hit them how seriously ill she was and they put her in hospital, it was too late, they said. Six days after she was admitted, she went to paradise. I thought it was for the best and felt relieved. But on the night of her wake, I was surprised how bitterly everyone was crying.

"If only she'd told us sooner it was so bad," Mother wept, "there might have been something they could do. I've never known such a good girl. She never disobeyed, she just went quietly about earning her keep. You should all learn a lesson from her!"

"So you'd be satisfied, would you," Karuta retorted, "if we all worked ourselves to death like Takemi?" Then she turned to me and said, "What fate brought her into the world? She was sacrificed by her parents and then by this greedy hag. I wonder if she ever enjoyed anything in her whole life!"

"What are you gawking at, Low? You're not even crying!" They could scold me, but Takemi had gone to the place she'd always said she wanted to go. She was at peace at last, so why should everyone carry on so? I found it all very strange.

THE HOT IRON

After Takemi died, Karuta behaved quite wildly. Before then, she'd never been one to come back drunk, but now she would come home dead drunk every night. "How can anyone live honestly in a world like this?" she would say. And when we'd tell her it was only ten o'clock or so, she'd pull the quilt over her head and go to sleep. Mother was furious and tried to drag her out and get her up, but she'd say, "I'm sick, I can't move." You couldn't budge her with a crowbar.

Mother was so angry she stuffed a snowball down the front of her kimono and finally pulled the kimono right off her.

"You, Low, and you, Hamako, fill the basin with water. I'm just going to cool her off a bit and bring her to her senses."

She forced us to hold the basin steady while she grabbed Karuta by the hair and pushed her face down into the water. But no matter how she was mistreated, Karuta would only go limp and refuse to resist or cry out. She glared at Mother with fury burning in her eyes. I was shaking with fright as I waited for Mother to leave.

Then I fussed over her, asking if it hurt and whether she wanted to put her kimono on. Karuta took me in her arms and hugged me gently.

"I'm all right. Don't worry," she said, stifling her sobs. On her feet were lots of little burn marks. They were scars where Mother had stubbed out her cigarettes.

One night I was asleep when Shizuka woke me up.

"Low! Get up! Your favorite Sister's having a dreadful time!"

Still half asleep, I raced up to the second floor. Mother was holding Karuta's feet down and pressing a hot iron against them. Karuta was gritting her teeth and glaring furiously at Mother. Without stopping to think, I blindly flew at Mother, screaming at the top of my lungs. In that same instant she shouted, "Shut up!" and knocked me flat on my back. Father was right behind me. Involuntarily I shrieked, "Help me! Please!"

Mother's eyes seemed glazed with rage as suddenly she flung me down the stairs. Oh no! That was my first thought, and then from within my leg the sound of bones cracking ripped through my brain.

When I came to, I was in a hospital room. I felt dreadful pain in my right leg and raised a howl of agony. Karuta was at my bedside, and she put her mouth to my ear.

"No matter what they do to you," she whispered, "the only way defenseless people like us can resist is by not resisting." It wasn't her leg, so she could talk that sort of happy nonsense. But I was in so much pain, I couldn't bear it. The doctor would pull and then push as if attempting to stick the broken bones in my leg back together again. I just couldn't endure any more pain, and I yelled at him.

"You dumb quack! Better you just wring my neck and get it over with!"

Karuta came to visit me every day, but except for her I was deserted. A splint had been strapped to my leg; I had a fever of 40 degrees [Celsius]; and I lay there all alone, enduring the pain. There was a call bell within reach, and as the nurse left she had said, "If you need anything, please ring."

It was about four or five days after I'd been admitted to hospital, I think. I woke up in the middle of the night needing to pee. The nurse was supposed to help me with that, but she didn't seem a very kind person and always made a face. Of course no one's going to like taking care of someone else's bottom, but . . . Anyhow, I did my best to hold on, somehow or other; but it was hopeless. I couldn't walk, so there was nothing for it but to get the nurse up. I felt for the bell, but it wasn't there. I looked around and there it was, hanging from the wall, illuminated by the dim light of a lamp. There was no way I could reach it without standing up. There was a wash basin in the hall; perhaps I could go there, I thought, and moving my right leg with both hands, bottom on the floor, I slowly edged toward the door. Halfway there, out it came. "Scolded again." I was resigned to it and dragged myself slowly back to bed, full of self-recrimination and unable to hold back my tears.

Next morning the nurse found out about it. "No matter how late it is, if you wake me up I'll come," she said, never bothering to mention that she'd forgotten to leave the bell within reach. She was scrubbing the tatami mats, which were thoroughly soaked with pee, with a vicious vigor.

After that, I decided that I'd eat only in the morning and never in the afternoon. If I ate something, I'd want a drink of water, and then I'd have to face the painful consequences in the middle of the night. Every time Karuta came to visit, she'd buy me something, but I didn't eat any of it.

THE SCAR

I told Karuta about my terrible experience, but her only response was a perfunctory "Oh really?" and then she was off home. But in the middle of that night, she quietly woke me up.

"Little Crane. Do you still want to go on living in this world? I've been thinking I'd take you with me and we could die together."

"If you're going to die, then I want to die too," I said. She undid her obi and tied me to her back, and together we went to Lake Suwa. There was no wind; the willow trees that lined the shore were still, the water black and calm.

Suddenly I said, "Not Lake Suwa. Anywhere else is fine, but not Lake Suwa." Stubbornly I insisted on having my way and began to cry. A dragon lived in Lake Suwa, it was said, and anyone who drowned would be mauled and the body would float to the surface. I was afraid of that dragon. Ignorant as I was, I believed there really was a dragon.

"All right, then. If you're that put off, let's try the railroad tracks." In an agony of indecision, she slipped off her wooden sandals and took them in her hand. "If we hurry we'll make the 12:05 for Tokyo," she said, heading for the tracks. "When you die on the railroad tracks, you mustn't look back, you know. If you look back, you'll lose your nerve." She hurried faster and faster. Even now I can't forget how terrified I felt. From out of the pitch dark, that black monster with one shining eye. Raising its voice in a roar, it came flying toward us.

Again I turned coward. I did mean to commit suicide, but when I began to think of the weight of that train on my body, it was too awful. Karuta stood jubilantly on the tracks, still supporting me on her back; I began to kick and struggle.

"Karuta, stop it! Please! Run! I'm scared! No!"

There she stood, stock-still as if she were dreaming. Was it the screams of the mad creature on her back that brought her round? At the last moment she jumped off the tracks. In that instant a blast of air hit my cheek, and the black engine roared, rocking our bodies as it passed. Karuta must have stumbled on something; she fell over, with me still on her back, and the pain in my injured leg made my head throb. When the train had passed into the distance, she spoke softly.

"Forgive me, Little Crane. I didn't do it because I wanted to die. It's just that I felt so sorry for you, getting you injured on my account and then leaving you all alone and making you suffer like that. I agonized for ages, and then I made up my mind. But if you don't want to die, then there's no reason for me to kill you. I'll earn as much as I can, and if there's a single sen I can keep secret from Mother, then I will. I'll spend it on you; I'll give something to the nurse to make things better for you, even if it's only a little bit." As she spoke, she trudged down the dark frosty road back to the hospital. She was eighteen, and I was twelve.

We had sneaked out of the hospital in great stealth, so no one ever found out what we'd done. But my leg was much worse from the fall, and a huge, ugly scar would remain for the rest of my life. I felt deeply ashamed of this scar, which is why, I suppose, I developed such an inferiority complex.

The next day I had a high fever, and the doctor shook his head in puzzlement. "That's strange," he said. "That's strange." My wound was so painful it throbbed with every beat of my heart. For three days I bore it; then I couldn't take it any longer and complained. The doctor took the plaster off.

"Damn. It's infected." He was so perplexed it was pitiful; and then they sent for the mistress of the Takenoya.

I LEARN MY NAME

What they decided then, I don't know, but my real mother was summoned, and I was admitted to the Suwa Red Cross Hospital. They took an X-ray; another day passed; then a nurse carried me in her arms into the operating room. My heart was pounding, and no matter how I clenched my teeth, I couldn't stop them chattering as I imagined the pain they were about to inflict on me. I felt an uncontrollable urge to pee. Outside the room I could hear the doctor shouting angrily. Amputate one leg—can't take responsibility—

why wasn't she brought in sooner—the girl crippled because of her parents' carelessness. My nerves were so on edge I could feel his voice pounding in my head.

I was anesthetized and don't remember anything after that. When I came to, my leg was wrapped in bandages. That night it bled horribly; they had spread five layers of newspaper and a sheet of oil paper under it; all of them were sticky with blood. The day after next, the gauze dressing was changed. It crackled when they took it off, probably because the blood had dried hard from the heat of my fever. The agony made me writhe so much that the next day the nurse gave me a strip of gauze.

"Put this in your mouth and bite on it," she told me. "If you cry out, it irritates the doctor and you'll be hurt even more." When the doctor came into the room, I decided to wait my turn with the quilt pulled up over my head.

On the fourth day, my mother said, "If I don't get back to work, everyone at home'll starve. I can't stay with you any longer. There's an invalid at home and four children waiting for me. I've asked the nurses to look after you, so do as they say and make them like you." She went home. We parted before I'd been up to calling her "Ma" even once.

There were six beds in the room and five patients. The child next to me was a boy of about my age, looked after by his grandmother; and next to him was someone looked after alternately by an old woman and an old man. This person, they said, had been in hospital for eleven years already. His whole body was covered with the scars of periostisis, and he couldn't move. He used a small hand mirror to look at whatever he wanted to see. The person in the bed behind mine had gone to help haul the "Sacred Pillar."[6] It had dropped on him and crushed his ankle, so they were going to have to amputate his foot. But he hadn't yet given up hope that something might be done, they said, and his wife was there with him. The Sacred Pillar is the tree trunk to which they attach a great hawser and haul through the town every seventh year during the Suwa Shrine Festival. The person next to him had had one of his kidneys removed, but he wasn't making a good recovery. He tottered about unsteadily, and every day he strummed at a battered old guitar.

Everyone sympathized with me, abandoned and all alone, and was very kind to me. The nurses, too, would wipe my face with a warm towel in the morning, help me eat, and if they had time, they would comb my hair, which had grown quite long by then. After about ten days, my temperature in the morning had returned to normal, and I could enjoy leafing through, over and over again, the comic books lent me by the child in the next bed.

Dr. Ishii said that with the quilt over me and only my leg protruding I looked just like a loach. Loaches, he said, burrow down into the mud whenever they sense danger; so he began to call me "Loach." It was Dr. Ishii who treated me the day I'd been admitted, when I'd hurled all manner of abuse at him. "Ouch! Enough! Get your hands off me you quack! Idiot! I'll scratch your eyes out, quack!" The others on my ward joked endlessly about this incident, pointing out that Dr. Ishii was deputy director of the hospital and a very skilled physician.

One day, as it happened, Dr. Ishii pulled at the quilt and said, "Come on now, Loach! No hiding yourself. Show us your face!" I held the quilt down with both hands.

"Didn't hurt a bit today, did it? Well, I've got a little something for you for not crying, so let's have a look, eh?"

Even then I clutched tightly at the quilt and refused to show myself. The nurse said, "Take it nicely now! Doctor says he'll give you a caramel, you know." At this I abruptly stuck one hand out, and he placed the caramel on my outstretched palm.

"Doctor's never done this before, you know," the nurse said. "You're a very lucky girl, Miss Masuda."

Being called "Miss Masuda" quite took my breath away. So my name wasn't "Nursie," wasn't "Crane," wasn't "Low"; it was Masuda. At the age of twelve, after coming to this hospital, I was told my name for the very first time.

CRUEL RULES

New Year's came and went, and I turned thirteen. Day by day my leg improved; everyone fussed over me, and I hadn't a care in the world. The charity ward in the hospital was paradise for me. For the first time in my life I was treated like a human being. Even if I was in pain, I desperately wanted to stay there just a little longer.

The man who'd had his foot crushed beneath the Sacred Pillar eventually gave in and had one of his legs amputated. Since only his ankle was damaged, he was saying, perhaps it'd be enough to cut off the leg below the knee. But what good is half a leg? It would only get in the way, they told him, and cut it off at the thigh. When he came back from the operation with only one leg, his mother and his wife wept bitterly.

One day Elder Sister Karuta turned up unexpectedly.

"Forgive me! I've been so worried about you, but Mother said you no longer had anything to do with the house, so I wasn't to visit you under any circumstances. Today I had a customer book me out and came in to see a movie. I pretended to go to the bathroom and slipped out. Are you all alone? Isn't anyone looking after you?" she asked. "How terrible! In such a filthy place!" she went on sympathetically. I told her that everyone was very good to me, that it was a fine place.

"At long last I've managed to get some money together without Mother finding out," she said, giving me 3 yen. Then she rushed off. I'd never had money of my own before and had no idea what to do with it. I found it quite bewildering.

The man who'd had his leg amputated looked at Karuta and asked me, "She's your elder sister, is she?"

I didn't know how best to reply. "Yes," I said, "she's not my real elder sister, but she's still my Elder Sister."

Then what's your connection? Did you live in the same house? And in this way the fact that I was a novice got out. All of them said the same things.

"What a pity this sweet child's to become a geisha! If only there were something we could do! And even you they put in the charity ward—dreadful!" They were even kinder to me than before.

Then, six days later, I was moved to a private room with tatami mats on the floor. The old woman came along to look after me, too. "Why have I been moved?" I asked the nurse. "When I wanted to stay where I was?"

"It has nothing to do with me. It was an order from the office."

I suppose it's because their duty stations were different, but the nurse was a different nurse too–and very brusque. I got her to call Nurse Kobayashi from the previous ward.

"Why have I been put by myself? Is it because I was disturbing everyone? But you know I never made a noise! And even when I was being treated and having injections, I didn't make a sound, did I? Please put me back where I was before!"

"You're a good girl. But from now on you're in the pay section. Where you were up till now is for people who can't pay."

"How is it I can pay now? Even if I can pay, please let me stay me where I was before. Please, ask the director of the hospital for me!"

"I can't do that. It's the rule. I'll pop in and see you when I've got a minute, so be a good girl like you were before."

But I'd been happy where I was! Why did they have to have these rules? And the money! Just because I have some, I'm robbed of the satisfaction of it. That, at any rate, was my view of the matter, and I was bitterly disappointed. The man with the guitar was going to get some sweet bean cakes from home and said he'd give me some! The man who'd had his leg amputated was going to be discharged soon, and he'd promised to give me the vase and the flowers from his bedside table! Everything I'd been looking forward to vanished like a dream.

Every morning and every evening, the old woman who was looking after me would twist her body and wave her hands in strange
ways, and chant, "Cleanse us of evil! Deliver us, we beseech thee!"
She told me to do it, too. Since she was the one who had to do everything for me, even wipe my bottom, I thought it best not to hurt her
feelings. I tried as hard as I could, lying in bed, to follow her.

After a few days had passed, Mother from the Takenoya and
Elder Sister Karuta came, and the mystery of how I was able to pay
was solved. Karuta had borrowed money by extending her contract; it was she who was paying the hospital bills. I felt the weight
of her goodwill fall heavily on me.

I DEVOTE MYSELF TO ART

My five months in the hospital came to an end, and I went back to
the Takenoya. That I was able to go back with both legs intact was
entirely due to Dr. Ishii. At the Takenoya, Elder Sister Hamako had
taken the professional name of Temari and had begun working as
an apprentice geisha on half-wages. All my Elder Sisters said the
same things:

"You've still got both legs! We'd heard from Mother that you
were going to have to have one leg amputated. So it really is true
that there are good doctors at big hospitals."

"But Mother really is horrid. Abandoning you like that when
she thought you wouldn't be any further use to her. Then when she
thinks she can get something out of you, she works you half to
death! She'll pay for this one day, you'll see."

They chattered on in this vein, trying to comfort me, perhaps,
or vent their anger. Of all of them, Karuta was the most sincerely
overjoyed.

"Dear Crane! Let's live together happily from now on. You and
I are true sisters," she said, putting her arm around my shoulders
and shedding a few tears.

My leg was a bit bent and bore a deep scar, but I had no difficulty getting to and from classes. No longer would I indulge myself with fond thoughts of how frightened I'd be if I were scolded, how much it would hurt if I were hit. I was completely driven by the desire to learn my art, become a fully fledged geisha, and help pay back the extra years Karuta had added to her contract. Of course even when I did start going to parties, as long as I was on "full keep," then all my earnings—no matter how much I might make—would go the geisha house; not a whit could be put toward reducing her contract. But I didn't know that yet. To become a fully fledged geisha—that, and that alone, was my heart's desire. Walking down the road, lying in bed, I would bend my body, move my fingers, determined not to forget my dance steps and shamisen fingering.

Chapter 3 &~ Miss Low Gets Wise

SHALLOW RIVER

In the spring of my fourteenth year, I made my long-awaited debut as an apprentice, and Elder Sister Temari became a fully fledged geisha. At this point I should explain something about how the geisha system worked in those days.

When you were sold, your approximate worth was calculated in *tama*, meaning "jewels," the euphemism used to describe the units in which geisha's wages were calculated. At most it would be 100 yen, although plain creatures like me would have fetched only 30 yen. At that time, 1 *shō* [1.8 liters] of polished rice cost somewhere between 20 and 22 sen, the same as a pair of *tabi* socks, as I recall; so in today's money that means I was sold for about 20,000 yen.

At first, novices learned their art, did chores around the geisha house, and were fed and clothed. When you became an apprentice, you started to attend parties, called *zashiki*, where you danced and served saké, but you didn't stay overnight. Your wages, called *gyoku-dai*, were only half, *han*, and that's why apprentices were known as *hangyoku*.

When you became a fully fledged geisha, there was an exam that was attended by the dance teacher and the shamisen teacher, your Mother and Elder Sisters from your geisha house, the head of the geisha association, the police, and the people from the geisha registry office. When you were sold, too, the police and someone from the registry office were called as witnesses.

The two years after you'd made your debut as a fully fledged geisha were on "full keep," *marugakae*: everything you made, both wages and tips, went to your house. And the house still provided your clothing and food. The two years after that, you were a "tip taker," *goshūgidori*, because the geisha house received your wages but you got to keep the tips. Your formal kimono were made for you, but you had to provide your own everyday wear.[1]

The length of a geisha's contract was determined when she was sold; ten years was the norm, and after the ten years were up, you worked one more year to show your gratitude. After that you were completely free, but mostly what happened was that you continued to work from the geisha house. You kept your wages and paid the house for room and board, plus a consideration for the loan of their name. But most girls were bought out by a patron as soon as they became fully fledged geisha and often became the patron's mistress, his "Number Two." Any geisha over the age of twenty was branded a has-been, and there weren't many of them.

This was a form of indentured service, which meant that if you were popular and sold well, the geisha house made money, and if you didn't, it lost. Girls who didn't sell well were "shifted," as the expression goes, and quickly sold to another geisha house.

Wages were passed from the restaurants to the geisha registry office, and from there they came to the geisha house. Nameplates for all the geisha hung in the registry office, arranged in order of popularity. On one side it said "free" and on the other, "engaged," so it was easy to see who was available. The restaurants didn't summon geisha directly from the geisha houses; everything had to go through the registry office.

On the day of my debut, I dressed up in all my finery and rode around town in a rickshaw, making calls on the restaurants and inns with someone from the registry office and Mother from the Takenoya.

When I started going to parties, I was more frightened of the older geisha than I was of the customers. Once one of them glared at you and said, "This one's a bit full of herself. Let's take her down a peg or two!" that was it. Suddenly, right in the middle of the party, you could be bullied in all sorts of ways. The song "Shallow River" was one of their favorite ways of tormenting apprentices.

> If the river is shallow,
> Lift your skirt to your shins,
> But when it gets deep,
> Then off comes your sash!

You'd dance while the older geisha sang; then on the last line, flip! You'd part your kimono and spin around.[2]

"What? That's the best you can do?" the older geisha would say, coaxing the customers to side with them. "Now let's see you do that again." The customers were only too happy to agree; and so once the evil eye had fallen on you, you'd be forced to do it all over again, two or three times or more. Most of the girls would burst into tears. I had that ugly scar on my leg and felt much more self-conscious than the others, but I was determined never to cry. My breast was a maelstrom of shame and humiliation; I felt I could shed tears of blood. But if you broke down and cried in a situation like that, it would only amuse the people who were trying to torment you. So I would respond with a grim smile as if to say, "If that's what you want, I'll give you as much as you like!" Once they realized they weren't getting anywhere, they'd try a different tack.

"I've heard from the mistress of the Takenoya that you're called 'Low.' I can see why!"

I'd pretend I didn't understand what they meant and nod in agreement. This may look as if I'd determined never to resist, no matter what they might do to me; but it may simply have been that I didn't possess the courage to protest, for I'd grown accustomed from an early age, albeit unconsciously, to knuckling under. They say that all living things, right down to the tiniest insects, have their methods of survival. Even the little inchworm knows how to camouflage itself to stay alive: it turns the same color as the tree, pretends to be a small branch, and. . . .

People said I was stupid, so I acted accordingly, not letting my feelings show, never contradicting others, pretending not to notice when something awkward happened, chatting politely about whatever seemed to please people.

When I could see that a customer was important to a particular geisha, I'd watch for a moment when no one else was near and then say something like: "Elder Sister's always talking about you, you know. She must really like you. I like you, too! And Sister likes you even more than I do. I guess that's what it feels like to be in love?" Then I'd flash him a big, innocent smile. Since they all were convinced that I was a bit weak in the head, they'd take me seriously and be really pleased. The customer would tell my Elder Sister. Elder Sister would feel flattered and start taking me with her to parties. And before long, all this effort began to bear fruit. I became popular.

A SECRET PLACE

Temari, who'd made her debut as a fully fledged geisha, was always making her customers angry and causing trouble. She'd abandon customers at a restaurant and run back to the house. Someone would come from the restaurant and try to patch things up. Mother would be furious and send Temari back to the restaurant. Then, long after she should have arrived, there'd come another reminder from the restaurant. Finally, she'd go missing altogether. Mother would tremble with rage, but there was nothing she could do. Finally she'd shout, "That little bitch! I'll bet she's run away. Perhaps I should report her to the police." She'd lash out at anyone and everyone who happened to be nearby. In that cramped house, we'd all creep away and do our best to stay out of sight. Then an hour or so later, word would come from the restaurant that she'd just arrived. The mistress of the restaurant would be furious and complain bitterly to Mother. "Never have I had to go to such lengths just to keep the customers from leaving. I'll thank you to be a bit more careful about this from now on!"

To be blacklisted by a restaurant was a huge loss to a geisha house, and it was humiliating. Mother would wait up, just aching to lay into her. "I'll give her hell when she gets back tonight!" she'd say. But Temari was a girl who knew what was what; on those nights, she wouldn't come back to the house. The next day, after she'd come back and heard all about the previous night's to-do, she'd tell us her side of the story, sometimes sprinkling her account with phrases from bawdy ballads.

"What a bore! How I detest that creep I had to see last night! He's been my patron since I made my debut, but. . . . He's got piles of money; but no matter how much money he's got, a disgusting man is still disgusting. There was something I wanted to think about, all by myself, so I sneaked out in the middle of the night and went to our secret place."

This secret place was a place only she and I knew about, just the two of us. The feudal domain of Suwa, rated at 30,000 *koku*, didn't rank high enough to plant pine trees, they say, so they planted zelkovas instead. The avenue leading up to the main gate of the castle, from the railway crossing all the way to the old ramparts, was lined on both sides with great zelkovas. Among them there was one huge tree that had grown a bit bent at the base of the trunk. From the time we were novices, we loved to climb up it and hide in the dense growth of leaves.

Temari went missing about once every two months. Even if I were at a party, when I heard that she had disappeared, I'd run straight to the bottom of the tree and call out to her in a soft voice.

"Is that you, Little Crane? Is Mother angry again?"

"Elder Sister! Come down!"

"I'm all right. I'm just having a cry now. Come up. Suwa looks lovely from a high place. Beautiful, just beautiful! I want to show you."

I'd tie back the long sleeves of my kimono and climb up; but I was much more elaborately dressed now than when I'd been a novice, so I couldn't just shinny up anymore. When I got there, though, I had to admit that it was a superb view. The city lights shone through the leaves, the people bustling about like so many ants. You could see the ruins of the castle. Beyond the Katakura Building, the water of the lake sparkled. I forgot I was supposed to come to fetch Temari and was almost transfixed myself.

"Nice, isn't it? The sadness, the pain, it all disappears. From now on, whenever you feel like it, climb up here and have a cry. When you're sad, I reckon, you've got to get up somewhere high and look down on the world." She was right; it really wasn't such a bad feeling—except for the difficulty of climbing up and down.

That night I was away from the party for about half an hour. The mistress of the restaurant scolded us severely, but Mother wasn't as hard on me as I'd expected.

"Just what are you two up to? Looking so sweet faced and pleased with yourselves! Well, I hardly dare show my face in that restaurant again. Try that once more, and I'll give your faces a press with the hot iron!"

But that was all. We were scolded so often that we had become hardened to it and didn't turn a hair at the occasional threat. When we were novices, she'd beat the shit out of us for the least little thing, but now we'd usually get off with a scolding. And as far as I was concerned, if I wasn't beaten, it didn't count as punishment; I was brazen.

From Mother's point of view, the fact that I was popular must have come as a great surprise, as if a beast she'd taken for a pack-horse had suddenly sprouted wings and flown off into the sky. But good-looking or not, once you've smeared on a bit of white make-up—assuming your face isn't on crooked—you'll be about as beautiful as anyone else. Whether you sell or don't sell depends entirely on your own efforts.

Mother was warm to those who were popular and cold to those who weren't, and the difference in treatment could be extreme. In the morning, very occasionally, she'd give each of us an egg in our soup, but if someone hadn't been engaged the previous night, she wouldn't get one.

"You didn't work last night, so you shouldn't be tired this morning, should you?" she'd say in front of everyone. At such times, my Elder Sisters would angrily mutter behind her back, "One measly egg! Who's dying to eat that? I'd rather smash it in Mother's face!" But no one was brave enough to say it in her presence. I never missed out on an egg, so I guess I was one of the "popular" girls.

Time passed, and one day Elder Sister Shizuka, whose favorite escape was still stories about Zenigata Heiji, was redeemed by her parents. And since it was her real parents who'd come to redeem her, there was nothing they could do about it; even Mother was powerless to prevent it. But this didn't mean that Shizuka could now go free. As a novice, she'd been sold on a ten-year indenture for 100 yen; add to that the cost of her training and her food, and she could be bought out for about 250 yen. But now that she'd become a fully fledged geisha, they could sell her to another house in a different locale where she'd be worth something like 300, maybe even 350, yen. Whatever the price, a chunk of that money would end up in her parents' pockets. They must have been rather badly pressed financially to have sold their own child in the first place. But parents who'll trade a child for money once will continue to try to wring money from her somehow or other. Once they hear that their daughter's become a fully fledged geisha, even if they don't sell her again, they're almost certain to turn up at least once or twice to wheedle a bit more money by extending her contract.

THE NEW NOVICE

The first New Year's Day after I became an apprentice I recall as being particularly lavish. It was 1940 or thereabouts. Big cities in China were falling one after another, and we all were carried away by it as if in a lantern procession at a festival. That must have been the peak of Japan's economic prosperity as well.

New Year's in the "flower-and-willow" district was excruciatingly beautiful. Everyone wore matching black-skirted kimono, white *tabi*, and black-lacquered sandals. Then we would tuck up the left side to reveal a flash of scarlet underrobe with each step, all to the gentle sway of elaborate Japanese coiffures. A geisha house that had five such beauties would line up five rickshaws and send them off around town to make New Year's greeting calls on their patrons. The patrons partied uproariously day and night. The amounts of money spent during that first week while the Gate Pines were on display were simply astounding. During that busy period and even after New Year's, I worked as hard as I could to earn as much as possible.

Spring arrived, and a new novice was sold to the Takenoya. When I caught a glimpse of her in the entryway, she was wearing a brand-new muslin kimono and wooden sandals with red thongs. Why was such a well turned-out girl being sold? It struck me as very strange.

After a bit, matters seem to have been concluded, and the girl stood in the entryway watching her father disappear from sight. I was shocked at the change in her appearance: now she looked even more ragged than I had when I first arrived at the house.

She sensed that I'd come up behind her and whirled to face me; her eyes brimmed with tears as she looked up at me imploringly. I smiled at her as if to say, "There's no need to be afraid of me." Poor thing! I'll look after you, I promise. In that instant, somewhere in my heart, I made that vow to her. "Give her a bath!" Mother told me, so I asked her all about herself while I was at it.

Her name was Michiko. She was fourteen years old and had just this year finished primary school. The clothes she'd been wearing when she arrived were borrowed from a neighbor; her father had taken them back with him, she said. Michiko was dressed in the same clothes I'd worn when I was a novice. When I thought of her, fated to suffer the same humiliation that I had, it filled me with pity. Today she knew nothing, she just felt lonely. But tomorrow it all would begin: day after day of burning anguish, of hiding herself away to cry in secret. I wanted to help her in any little way that I could.

By that time, Elder Sister Takechiyo had worked out her contract and was paying the house for the use of their name. Takechiyo liked to lord it over the others, so Michiko was bound to be tormented. Once I had become an apprentice and begun to sell, no one could mistreat me any more. For my own part, I never disobeyed anyone; I just worked as hard as I could to earn money.

After Michiko arrived, whenever I was at a party and I was told to go and fetch cigarettes from the counter for everyone, the older geisha included, I'd take an extra pack and hide it in my sleeve if I thought I could get away with it. Then after we got back, when Takechiyo would tell Michiko to go out and buy cigarettes in the middle of the night, I'd give them to Michiko and say, "Here, take these, go out to the tobacconist and pretend you bought them, then give them to her when you get back!"

And if I'd done the rounds of two or three parties, I'd always manage to earn a packet or two of chocolates or caramels. When you're an apprentice, if a customer says to you, "I'll buy you whatever you like. What do you want?" you mustn't ever say, even as a joke, that you want a diamond ring or something expensive like that. You have to say, in the sweetest possible voice, "sponge cake" or "chocolate," or they won't be at all pleased. All the chocolates and caramels I earned like this I gave either to little Fusa, the nursemaid at the hairdresser I used, or to Michiko. Little Fusa was sure to be hungry, I thought, remembering how hungry I'd always been when I was a nursemaid.

At that time, there was a very strange customer who claimed he was Saigō Takamori.[3] We called him "Mr. Sai." He never once summoned fully fledged geisha, but he would sometimes hire two or three apprentices, take us to the Shirokiya department store, and buy us new collars for our underkimono or ornaments for our hair. He'd parade through town with us in broad daylight, and on days when there was horse racing, he'd pile us into a chauffeured car and take us to the track. He never placed any bets for himself, but he took great delight in betting on our behalf. He'd turn up only once a month or so, but whenever he did, I'd get him to buy me red *tabi* for winter or whatever else I thought little Fusa might like.

THE SLEEP-WITH-ANYONE GEISHA

Toward the end of that year, a new geisha moved in. On the day she arrived at the Takenoya, Father asked her, "What's your name?" I'm told she simply shrugged her shoulders and said, "Name? I don't have a name. I thought you were supposed to give me one!"

She'd made her debut under the name Sennari, but from the evening of the day she arrived, she slept around here, there, everywhere, and hardly ever slept at the house. We used say of a geisha who'd sleep with anyone that she'd "fall into bed without looking."

For in those days, a geisha who was considered "first class" would-n't sleep with just anyone. As soon as they made their debut, most geisha were fixed up with a *danna*, or patron. If he was good to you, you'd have only one; but if he was stingy and you found it difficult to cover expenses, you'd have two or three *danna*, and you would-n't sleep with anyone else. All of this would be arranged secretly be-tween the Mother of your house and the people at the geisha reg-istry office. Then the inns and restaurants would be informed that "so-and-so has a *danna*, so she doesn't do overnight stays."

When your *danna* arrived, you didn't just disappear with him right away; you engaged two or three other geisha and made a party of it. You didn't snuggle up to him coquettishly or anything like that but poured drinks for him with proper ceremony. Then you'd go to a different room, have one of the maids undo your obi for you, and give her a tip. A geisha slept in her underkimono, but an apprentice from your house would bring an everyday kimono for you to wear home the next day, taking back the formal kimono that you'd worn at the party.

Without some very good reason, you didn't sleep with anyone other than your *danna*. But when you did do it, a clever geisha would never sleep with someone local but would choose someone her *danna* couldn't find out about, such as a traveler. To be suc-cessful at this sort of thing, you had to keep constantly in the good graces of the mistresses of the restaurants and their maids. Other-wise it could prove disastrous if you had to see two *danna*, one right after the other.

When a customer asked for you by name, even though your nameplate at the geisha registry office indicated that you were "en-gaged," he would be put "on hold" (*naka-morai*). If he insisted on you and you alone, he was put on "priority hold" (*zehi-morai*). If two *danna* wanted you at the same time in different restaurants, it could happen—rarely, to be sure—that you would sleep first with the one "on hold" and then come back to the first one. When that happened, you'd come in saying something like, "So many people at that other party! I'm exhausted!" and make a show of mopping the sweat from your brow. I learned all this later after I'd become a fully fledged geisha; but if you were going to put someone "on hold" while you went off to sleep with someone else, you had to turn on the charm as soon as you got there to get him in the mood, which required plenty of guile and all manner of clever tricks.

A full banquet went like this: in the first round, the geisha would sing and play the shamisen and drums while the apprentices danced; then the Elder Sisters themselves would dance. After about two hours, there'd be a break, and the customers who were going home would leave. Then there'd be a second round of partying. After that you'd take a bath, and everyone would go off to their separate rooms to sleep. On these occasions, the geisha would sleep with their set *danna*, and the sleep-arounds would make up the numbers if there weren't enough of us to go around.

Of her own accord, Elder Sister Sennari became a sleep-around geisha from the very start. The other geisha seemed not to like it; they all ignored her, as a result of which Sennari herself stubbornly refused to let anyone get close to her. She'd go the whole day without speaking to anyone, and—perhaps it was some sort of lucky charm—she'd take a silver 50-sen coin out of an amulet case she kept at her waist, place it on the palm of her hand, and stare intently at it.

We were in the habit of bathing after the morning cleaning was done. One day, when we all were in the bath, Takechiyo said to Sennari, somewhat sarcastically, "You shouldn't overdo it, you know. It's not healthy."

"Much obliged to you, I'm sure! But is it such a great inconvenience to you, whatever I might do with my own body?"

Then Temari opened her mouth. "You'll give the Takenoya a bad name, that's what!"

Sennari was in the middle of washing her hair. She tipped the whole basin of water over Temari and said, "What the hell are you talking about? And every one of you doing the same thing yourselves! If he's not your husband, what's the difference between having one man and having ten?" She spat out the words as she stood up and left without even drying herself. Temari let out a scream and made as if to chase after her. "I'll tell Mother about you!"

"Just a minute now," Karuta stopped her. "If you tell Mother she won't side with you, you know. This is an argument between colleagues, and there's no need to say a word to Mother."

"Karuta," Takechiyo chimed in, "you're stupid to stick up for Little Sen like that! Is there any good reason?"

"Elder Sister Takechiyo—just how many years have you lived in the flower-and-willow world? You shouldn't have provoked her like that! No one likes having their weak spots pointed out; it's no wonder she got angry."

Sennari was forgotten as the two of them got into a huge fight, neither willing to give way to the other. I hardly knew what to do, when Mother arrived. "If you enjoy fighting so much, then fight the whole day long, see if I care!" She shut them both in the bath and barred the door from the outside.

I was so fond of Karuta, I ran straight to Sennari. "All because of you, Karuta's been shut up in the bath. Please," I begged her, "you've got to do something!" She was gazing sadly at her 50-sen coin again, but she went to the bath, unbarred the door, then tripped back to her room.

Mother's certain to punish her for that, I thought; and sure enough, it wasn't long before she was summoned. But the angrier Mother became, the more sullen Sennari was.

"If you don't like me, then sell me, I couldn't care less! One place is the same as another," she shouted. I was shocked how bold she was. But when Mother let her go, and she went back to her room and lay down with the quilt over her head as if she were asleep, I knew she was crying.

"Who does she think she is?" Temari muttered, "The beast!" But I couldn't agree. Until now, I'd disliked her, but from then on, I vowed that I'd do my best to get along with her.

How to be cute and sexy

Soon it would be my turn to become a fully fledged geisha, so I devoted myself eagerly to the preparations. It wouldn't do to play the ingénue forever. I had to study how to make them feel that I was cute and sexy.

First, you watch a customer's face and wait until your eyes meet. The moment your eyes meet, you flutter your eyelashes two or three times, then lower your eyes, and look at him again. If your eyes meet this time, then you've timed it just right. You'd think that the next step would be to blush attractively, but it doesn't work like that. You have to pretend that your cheeks are blushing uncontrollably, put your hands to your face, stand up, and rush out into the corridor. Whenever I had time, I practiced this in front of the mirror.

Elder Sister Takechiyo would make fun of me. "That's disgusting!" she'd laugh. "The child thinks she's become a woman and spends all her time in front of the mirror!"

"That's not true!" I'd protest, in all seriousness. "I'm practicing for when I make my debut!"

"That's right, Little Crane," Temari said. "After you make your debut, everything's different, even the way you greet people. Let me show you. See? It's like this." Then she'd show me how to do it, with all the gestures. I suppose she must have learned by watching the others; but when she was talking to customers at a party, she made even another women like me shed a tear or two with her ability to charm and flirt.

I decided I'd copy what she did, but I couldn't do it nearly as well. Still, once I'd got it to the "this-might-just-do" stage, I tried it out, starting on customers who looked like they might be vulnerable. It was a huge success! If I ran into one who'd reacted in the corridor, he'd put his arm around my shoulders. I'd make a show of protesting, "No! Let me go! Don't frighten me like that!" But at the same time, I'd leave him with the sense that maybe I didn't find it so very bad after all.

Around that time, it seems to me that my true nature began to reveal itself. Whether or not I was short of brain, I don't know, but I was certainly no ingénue. I was convinced that mastering these arts was essential to my survival; the thought that they might be despicable never so much as crossed my mind. This was when I was still only fifteen years old. Little by little, I'd begun to sense just who might be maneuvering to become my *danna*.

Chapter 4 🦋 Bird in a Cage

MY FIRST CUSTOMER

After the New Year's festivities of my sixteenth year, I made my professional debut. On that day, at the behest of those customers who had taken an interest me and some of the customers of my Elder Sisters whom I knew, I put in an appearance of twenty or thirty minutes, after which I left for a party given by the person who was to become my own *danna*, or patron.

My *danna* was a man nicknamed "Cockeye." His eyes were squinty, he was going bald, and his face glowed bright red; when he sat drinking in his quilted cotton jacket, dripping with sweat and leering with satisfaction, he looked just like an octopus. And what was really creepy was that you could never tell where he was looking. But I wasn't a bit afraid, nor did I feel the least bit sorry for myself. I racked my brains for ways I might get him to like me, ways I could keep him for a long time.

I had heard stories about Cockeye before. He was a small-time promoter and gang boss, they said, and very fond of virgins. He'd had the first taste of most of the geisha, apparently, but only that once, they said. "Hasn't a penny to his name, that bum," Karuta had told me.

Even since my apprentice days Cockeye had been somewhat excessive with his attentions, and I sensed that he had designs on me; but I'd never dreamed he would be my first.

Mother had taken my hands and shown me quite specifically what I was to do with them during my "initiation." And my Elder Sisters would often tell me things like "they love it if you nibble at their ears." I learned quickly from these conversations, and once we got into bed it was me who made the first move. It wasn't a matter of liking it or disliking it; I was just determined that I would get him to like me. What can I say? This too, sadly, becomes second nature to a geisha.

Next morning Cockeye laughed and said, "You're as bold as thirty women. I thought I'd been fed a load when they told me this was your first time; but yeah, you're a virgin all right."

Thereafter, Mother sold my "first time" to four more men, one after another, and made a pile. Every time she would give me my lessons all over again, in the most tedious detail. "Now you don't say anything about your previous *danna*. Have you got that?" And again she would teach me all the virgin-like gestures I was to make. I just kept quiet and bent myself to her will.[1]

From then on, I, who knew nothing of the value of money, was launched on the sort of life that could be bought and sold for money. So long as she's selling well, the child of a foot soldier could live as selfishly as the daughter of a great lord. Even when customers said they would buy me a little something or offered to give me some pocket money, I got them to credit it to my earnings. If you could build up a bit of leeway, then you didn't have to go to parties when you didn't feel like it, and no one would complain if you lay around napping at home.

Elder Sister Karuta used to teach me things. "Customers are children and geisha are chestnuts," she would say, "so you mustn't just pop out of your shell of your own free will and say, 'Oh, do come in.' If they don't have to make a bit of an effort, you won't seem so delectable. But if they think there's something delicious inside that shell, they'll do anything to get at it, even if they have to bloody their hands on the burrs. So sometimes it's a good idea to prick them with your thorns. Something they've gone to that much trouble to get hold of, they'll respect; they won't take you for granted. You've got to use your wits." It isn't just us geisha, I thought, all women ought to take this admonition to heart.

Had I gone on for long just as I was then, knowing hardly anything of love and affection, never mistrusting the world; had it never occurred to me to reflect on my own past, then I might have gone through life free of care, with no turmoil or grief.

The geisha temperament

As I said before, the old "flower-and-willow" district had certain rules that had developed naturally over the years. And as geisha, we had a certain pride.

Karuta was a first-rate Elder Sister: she had standards and would never sleep with any man other than her *danna*. This was not from a sense of feminine virtue; it was a sad sort of pride. This "geisha's pride" wasn't worth a broken straw sandal, of course, but—under the influence of Karuta, I suppose—its hollow conceits took root in my mind.

Geisha with standards of this sort don't snuggle up coquettishly to customers or anything like that. We practiced other, more refined techniques for conveying the same sexiness. Besides, most of our customers were urbane people. If their behavior grew indecent, they'd cut it out if you told them, "When you make jokes like that, I begin to wonder what sort of man you are!"

In this world, the most disloyal thing you could do was to sleep with another geisha's *danna* knowing full well who he was. So if he tried to talk you into it, you'd put him off tactfully by saying, "Oh, you must be joking! You of all people must know that I could never do anything so disloyal. Please don't tease us when we're in no position to refuse." But some men wouldn't go along with this. And if the geisha who had previously been bought by the man found out about it, then three or more of them would gang up on you and give you a dreadful going-over.

There was one time when I didn't realize that one of my customers was the *danna* of a geisha named Kingo. The geisha were horrible to me. Amid a crowd of customers, the sarcasm began: "This one says she'll do it for two points. If anyone wants her, just take her in the next room."

Normally, when you stayed the night with your *danna*, he paid only for your time; and when you spent the night with someone who wasn't your *danna*, you received double points; and when you just slept with a customer without staying the night, it was ten points; so "two points" was a real insult.

"She says she doesn't mind if you're someone's *danna*."

" 'Whore' fits her better than 'geisha,' don't you think?"

"In our world, I really wish those who have no sense of honor wouldn't pretend to be geisha."

"Elder Sister Crane's a first-class 'artiste,' really!"

"Elder Sister Crane, could you play the shamisen for me? I'd like to be permitted to dance. Please?" she said, pleading with both hands to the floor. To be called "Elder Sister" by a geisha senior to oneself cuts like a thorn. Besides, the shamisen is always played by the senior geisha, and it's the junior ones who dance.

I burst into tears and ran wailing up to the counter. "Mother! She said I'd do it for only two points!" I moaned, clinging to the knees of the mistress of the restaurant. "I just couldn't bear to stay in there any longer."

"Hopeless! At her age, bullying a young thing like you! Don't worry about today. You go on home," she said, sending me on my way.

When I got home, the minute I saw my Sisters' faces, I complained tearfully to each of them. It seems to be human nature to protect the weak, but women of this world especially I could always count on, even knowing nothing of the situation, to take my side as long as I appealed to them in tears. Even Elder Sister Takechiyo, to whom I was not especially close, began planning a payback with Elder Sister Karuta.

At long last, revenge. This was the day everyone was determined to pay her back, two or even three times over. We called Elder Sister Kingo to a banquet. Just as the first session was coming to a close, we began, one after another.

"Gentlemen, today we have a special favor to ask of you all. Three years have passed since Elder Sister Kingo became a fully fledged geisha, and now her one and only *danna*, that she worked so hard to find, has jilted her for a younger girl."

"At the moment she is in search of a new *danna*, so if any of you should have aspirations of this sort, please do let us know. We'll arrange everything to your satisfaction."

"Such youth, such beauty, such a shame that she should have no *danna*. We, for our part, just can't let the matter pass."

Elder Sister Kingo responded. "I'm most grateful to be the recipient of your kind concern, but I'm not at all short of *danna*."

"Well then, Elder Sister Kingo! We've underestimated you. Sleeping around a bit, eh?"

"I beg your pardon! You're getting back at me for Miss Crane, I suppose; but all I did was warn her because she did something unbecoming of a geisha."

"Unbecoming of a geisha, you say? What might that be?"

"Grabbing someone else's *danna*, that's what!"

"Oh, really! May I inquire of you then: just what do you think we happen to be? But of course a top-class lady like yourself, Elder Sister Kingo, who has a proper *danna*, can live without grubbing for points. You're probably unaware of it, but we're for sale; and if we run short of money, that's it! The end!" On we all went in this vein.

"If Little Crane had bought off your *danna* with money, well then, we'd understand your anger."

"Suppose we buy a cotton kimono, and then we decide we don't like it. When we take it back, does the kimono get angry? Is that your story?"

"If you don't like us grabbing your men, then perhaps you should give up being a geisha; perhaps you could become a housewife and just look after your husband?"

"Grabbing? Grabbed? Well, not till this very moment have I known such words to pass the lips of a top-class geisha!"

Finally Elder Sister Kingo fled, weeping bitterly. At this point there was nothing that the mistress of the restaurant could do. If she had been so foolish as to open her mouth and take sides, the row would spread like wildfire.

Even if another geisha gets a bit too friendly with her *danna*, a wise geisha handles the matter lightly. Without changing her facial expression, indeed even amiably, she says, "Oh, so-and-so-san, you've been minding my place for me? I'm so sorry! I've been tied up elsewhere. *Danna*, give her a nice tip, won't you?" And that's the end of the matter.

MISCARRIAGE

I had turned seventeen when Michiko took the name Tsukiko and made her debut as a fully fledged geisha. It was just after the war with America began.

At the time of Tsukiko's debut, I was away on a trip. Cockeye, who was famous for being dreadfully possessive, had for some reason decided quite openly that he would become my *danna*. When he'd go on a trip, he'd sometimes book me out for the whole day, twenty-four hours straight, and take me along. It was on these trips that the true misery of being a body for sale really hit me. It was obvious to anyone—such was the difference in our ages—that we couldn't even be parent and child; I was young enough to be his granddaughter. And yet Cockeye would speak to me quite nonchalantly as if he were my husband. I did my best not to say anything in front of others and made myself as inconspicuous as possible.

I got back on the third day after Tsukiko's debut; she'd lost a lot of weight and looked as if she'd aged about three years.

"Tell me, Elder Sister Crane, when we make our debut, it's like an ordinary woman getting married, right? But when you get married, you get a place in return where you can live in peace; we get nothing! We just become someone's toy. Don't you think that's miserable?"

"So what if I do? You'll feel better if you don't think about things you can't do anything about." Back then, I found it tiresome the way people who'd been to school always had to debate everything.

Time passed, and after the flower-viewing season was over, I realized that I was pregnant. Damn! What was I going to do now? I went to ask Elder Sister Karuta's advice.

"You know, there's nothing so pitiful as the sight of a geisha who's pregnant. You can't dance with that big belly. What you do is go to the Inari Shrine by the station every day for twenty-one days. Vow that you'll donate a lantern if you miscarry. And every day, whenever you have a chance, try jumping off the edge of the verandah."

From the very next day, I did as I was told. Miracle or not, I couldn't say, but on the morning of the twentieth day, when I was getting ready to go out to the shrine, I felt a sudden pain in my abdomen. "So this is it," I thought, bracing myself against the pain.

The creature that should have been born as my child had turned into a mess of blood and miscarried. Everyone seemed to know about it, but no one did anything for me. Karuta cleaned up afterward and offered to call a doctor, but I didn't want anyone to find out. I just stayed in bed for two days and then started going back to parties. I didn't stop bleeding for fifteen days.

While I was lying in bed, Elder Sister Sennari came up and began earnestly to talk to me.

"You've had a miscarriage, haven't you? I knew what was going on. Everyone in this house—no, everyone in the world, I hate them all. But you're the only one I neither like nor dislike. Everyone calls me a sleep-around and looks down on me, but they're doing the same thing themselves. You don't seem to, though, do you?"

The reason I'd been faithful to Cockeye since he'd become my patron was because Mother had told me, "He's an important man, so you'd better not take any other customers." I'd simply done as I was told.

Sennari began to tell me about herself. "I finished school when I was fourteen, and right after that I was sent into service at a fishmonger's in Kawasaki. I'll never forget the fourteenth of December, when his wife took the children to her parents' for a visit. That same night the old man had his way with me. Even when you're sold as a geisha, they leave you alone until you're sixteen, but I was only fourteen! Don't you think that was cruel? Then he gave me 50 sen and told me not to tell anyone. It was this 50-sen coin here." She held out the 50-sen coin she was always staring at.

"All my dreams, all my hopes, snatched away for 50 sen! I ran away, straight back home to Shizuoka. But in those days I didn't have any courage, and I was too embarrassed; I just couldn't tell anyone that I'd run away because I'd been had by that old man. I just cried and cried. After that I went into service with a watchmaker in Tokyo; but maybe I just look like a slut because the guy who was the watchmaker's assistant kept making moves on me, and so I ran away again. Well I was damaged goods already, and I thought it'd help my family; so I sold myself as a geisha. I'm getting my revenge on men now. I've got two or three that'll go bankrupt any day now! Besides, there's nothing else I can do but sleep around, I'm no good at any of the geisha arts."

She smiled bitterly. It was a strange thing to do, I thought, avenging your Kawasaki enemy in Suwa; but if that was what gave her satisfaction, I saw no reason I should butt in. I listened to her story in silence.

THOU SHALT NOT LOVE

Rumors began to circulate that Elder Sister Karuta was in love with a young man. Mother was furious. "What an idiot that Karuta is! She knows what's what and who's who in this world! She ought to be ashamed of herself, falling in love with some boy and becoming the talk of the town for it. So she sees lover boy's face and that's enough to fill her gut? She can live for three or four days without eating? Well let her try eating nothing, then, starting today! A geisha who owes everything she has to me finds herself a lover boy—I suppose that makes her think she's really something."

After that, Karuta came home drunk again, and Mother laid into her; but no matter how hard she was hit, she'd only say, "Do what you like—see if I care!" Never would she apologize. Once she dug in her heels she wouldn't retreat an inch; she'd hold her ground right to the bitter end. Just watching her was as painful as if my own flesh were being cut.

"Elder Sister, you've got to apologize. Please, I beg you! Be the sister you used to be. If you need money, I'll get some from my *danna* and give it to you. If you make Mother angry, you'll be sold to another place!"

"It's all over anyhow. Mother's fixed it so we can't meet anymore. She says I spent money on him, when all I did was pay the restaurant bill for him three times. Maybe I should just run away!"

There were plenty of geisha who had run away, but the police always picked them up immediately; not one of them had ever managed to get away, even for two days. It would just be one more humiliation on top of all the rest.

"I wouldn't care even if I didn't get away! I'm past caring. Just because there's one person I happen to like, I'm treated like a criminal. I've had enough. Being in love is proof you're still alive."

In the end, she was sold to another house, even though she would have served out her contract by the end of the year. I prostrated myself in front of Mother and begged. "Mother, please, I beg you! I'll earn Elder Sister's keep on top of my own; please, do anything, but please don't move her to another house!"

But Mother wouldn't listen. "There's nothing more I can do for that shameless wretch!"

Then I went and pleaded with Karuta. "Elder Sister! Change your mind and go and apologize to Mother. Please, you've got to do something so you can stay here. If you don't want to work anymore, I'll put half my earnings down to your name, so please, stay with me!"

"Little Crane. This doesn't mean that our bond as Sisters will be broken. When the day comes that we both can be free, we'll live together. My heart and your heart, they'll always be joined. But you mustn't ever fall in love, you know. You'll be jeered at, and the whole world will look gray. There'll be a big hole in your heart with a cold wind blowing through it. And you'll be the only one to suffer. I want to go somewhere far away for a while. Forgive me, Little Crane, please."

The night before Elder Sister was to be sold, we got under the same quilt and cried the whole night through about the sad fate of humankind. Mother had said we "knew what was what and who was who in the world," but we'd been shown only the underside; we knew nothing about the good side. We'd been born into this world but knew nothing about what the sincere affection of a man might be. You make a rich *danna* spend money on you like hot and cold running water, but is that love? When someone who's starved of love is shown something that looks like sincere affection, is it any wonder that she jumps at it and clings to it? After all, we all were about twenty years old, we were women; so was it such a crime to dream of loving and being loved? But in our world, that sort of logic got you nowhere.

Perhaps even I was not entirely lacking a "woman's heart." I might happen to meet a stranger and feel my heart beat faster. I'd sing and dance, and we'd go our separate ways, yet I'd somehow feel depressed about it; and if I had to meet Cockeye after that, the feeling of desolation would be even greater. At such times, I'd climb up to that secret place and stay there all alone until very late.

In every human heart is a place where you put your broken dreams. When something doesn't work out, no matter what it may be, you just have to give it up and stuff it in with your broken dreams. And make sure you keep the lid on tight.

IN THE PARTY BUSINESS

I did my best to live by that creed of resignation, but in the geisha business it isn't enough just to do as you're told; you have to make a real effort. To make everyone, everywhere in your presence, feel that you're sexy requires constant care and attention. And when you appear before a customer for the first time, you have to work out at a glance what type of woman he likes. If you sense that he likes, say, the sweet and helpless sort, you have to adapt yourself quickly to his expectations.

Then, too, even though I hadn't been even to primary school, I'd never have got on if I hadn't been able at least to give the impression that I understood what customers were talking about, whether it was literature, politics, or whatever. I couldn't even read the *kana* syllables properly, much less more complicated characters;

rather, I had to be able to learn difficult words just by hearing them. If some such subject came up at a banquet, I'd pretend that I was just drinking saké and having a good time while actually I was concentrating my entire energies on the conversation; I'd memorize what they said and then repeat it at a different party. If people got carried away and the conversation threatened to develop into something a bit too deep, then just before they got off onto a topic I didn't know anything about, I'd say something like, "Let's not talk about anything so difficult here! Come on everybody, I'll dance, so why don't you all sing along?" Otherwise you could end up in a really embarrassing situation. You can't switch off, even for a moment. Like a tautly strung bow, you keep your mind alert and ready as you move with the flow, from banquet to banquet.

Geisha can do horrid, spiteful things: they'll attack one another tooth and nail, each trying to force the other out of the way. To someone who doesn't know this world and sees only the surface of it, I suppose we must appear quite carefree; but inwardly we're eternally weeping tears of pain and sorrow.

Before long, a letter addressed to me from Elder Sister Karuta, who'd gone to Chiba, arrived at a restaurant called the Ichiriki. I had the mistress of the Ichiriki read it to me. There was one difficulty after another in this new and unfamiliar locale, she wrote; but there was a man who said he would buy out her contract, so she was intending to go ahead with that.

The mistress of the Ichiriki was only thirty-four or thirty-five, but she once had been a geisha herself and had suffered terribly to get where she was, so she was kind to us in all sorts of ways.

There are people like this wherever you go, but just suppose a group of, say, three young men hire a geisha and tell her, "It's exhibition day!" or "We're going to play gynecologist!" They strike up a rhythm and start to undo her obi. All three of them gang up on her and hold her down; then one of them tries something utterly shameful. The geisha screams for help. In a situation like this, the mistress of the Ichiriki would immediately come running to her aid.

"My! My! What goes on here? A geisha, you know, has no one to protect her. I should think you'd feel sorry for her and treat her gently."

"What the hell are you yammering about? Just when things were getting interesting! Go on back to your account books!"

"Oh, go away, you say? Well, just for record, let me tell you: the one thing I don't allow here is customers who make the geisha scream, OK? Because it disturbs the other customers. If you insist on playing these perverted games, I'll take her away. Is that understood?"

"We've paid good money for her; we're not taking any orders from you, you old bag. Piss off!"

"What's that you say? I suppose you think you can behave like boors just because you're guests here! So full of yourselves! Well, this room and the saké are mine; the money is yours. Whether I sell or don't sell is entirely up to me. I've had enough of you filthy bastards with your filthy games! Get out!"

"You don't have to tell us to get out—we're gone! And we'll never be back!"

"Much obliged to you, I'm sure! Forgive me for being so bold as to say this, but foul-mouthed customers the likes of you guys are not welcome here. So off with you; get lost!"

"Yeah, we've heard all about you. It's a lot easier to worm money out of guys who're soft on women, isn't it?"

"What the hell are you talking about? Damned idiots! If you're feeling so sorry for yourselves, why the hell don't you go and buy out a first-class girl; show the world what a beauty you've got locked away in your garden? But I'll bet you'd be hard put to come up with 50 sen among you!"

In the end, what with all the wrangling and bickering, the money they were supposed to pay would be lost. At such times, you'd feel so embarrassed and so grateful that all you could do is mumble, "Mother, it's all my fault! Forgive me!"

"Never mind," she would laugh, " 'the more of them you burn, the more fallen leaves the wind will blow your way.' We're not on the brink of starvation yet. So long as people have mouths, they'll have to eat three times a day."

So we geisha would bring our *danna* who had called us to other restaurants over to her place once in every three times, and the Ichiriki did a roaring trade.

TIP TAKER

When I turned eighteen, Cockeye spoke to Mother about buying out my contract. Mother was ready for him: "But *danna*, that's just too cruel. . . . I've worked so hard and so long; then just when I can start presenting her in public. . . . No, I really can't part with her just now. . . . Besides, she's my favorite little girl, you know." She put on a great show of her unwillingness. In the end it was decided that for the rest of the year she would continue to send me to parties but that I would become a "tip taker."

For the first time in my life, I had money of my own to spend as I wished. No matter what you do, everything depends on how well you manage your money. The money I received as tips I used to improve my standing in the quarter, sharing it with the maids at the restaurants.

When I wanted to buy something, I would work on Cockeye's competitive instinct and squeeze it out of him. Elder Sister so-and-so had received a gorgeous formal kimono or a watch from *danna* so-and-so, I'd tell him. Or *danna* so-and-so was always *so* stingy with Elder Sister so-and-so that everyone was laughing at her, saying, "For a geisha with a *danna* to be so badly dressed—he must be terribly tight with his money. They wonder that he isn't embarrassed by it, but I really feel sorry for her." Things like that I'd say to him. You mustn't make these remarks as if you're gossiping maliciously; you have to give the impression that it's just innocent chatter with no ulterior motive.

This much was easy. But girls who had knocked around in the quarter for two or three years would use a different technique on every man. You had to know how to laugh when you were sad and cry when you felt like laughing.

Back then, I was earning more than two hundred points a month, but as I grew more confident, I became more and more willful. If a customer started pawing me, I'd stand up and say, "If you please, I'll take my leave now. I don't need these one or two points." When I did that, some people actually liked it and began to ask for me especially. It showed real character, they said; my nerve made me more interesting.

Cockeye explained the reason he wanted to buy out my contract like this: "It's because you've got guts. I hate people who don't have guts. Suppose you throw a rope to someone who's fallen down a deep hole and try to help them. There'll be some who grab the rope and haul themselves up, and others who're too weak and can't make it. The ones with guts will crawl up and walk away on their own two feet. I can't stand wasting my own efforts; I wouldn't give a gutless bastard even a single stalk of straw." I'm not so sure that I did have guts, but I know for certain that I was spiteful to the core.

Speaking of this reminds me of something else that happened. Elder Sister Temari and I used to wear the same size *tabi*, and whenever I'd wash a pair and fold them up, she'd wear them, get them dirty, and leave them lying about. I'd wash them without ever complaining, but after I began to sell and could do as I liked, I hid every last pair. Then when she was called to a party she'd panic.

"Little Crane! Do you know where my *tabi* are?"

"How should I know? I'm not your maid."

Even if we were called to a party together, I'd get myself ready and set off alone, pretending I knew nothing about them. She would arrive late and reproach me bitterly. "You're not very nice. Mother was cross with me!"

"Was she?" I'd say, feigning ignorance. "I guess you'll have to be more careful from now on, won't you?" I'd been wanting to get even with her for ages. Serves you right! It felt good.

TSUKIKO'S SUICIDE

Tsukiko was always in tears. "It's my fate," she would cry, no matter what it was that had happened. But then suddenly, she seemed bubbling with joy. Perhaps she's grown a little more accustomed to the geisha life at last, I thought.

"Elder Sister Crane," she said, utterly in rapture. "I'm going to get married!"

"Married? You mean for real?" I asked her.

"Of course. Hii-san says he'll buy me out and marry me! So I'm not going to listen to what anybody says except him. Mother can get as angry as she likes; I don't care if all my *danna* give me the sack! 'Cause I'm going to be bought out, maybe only two or three months from now!"

What a bewitching word *marriage* is! Sometimes, going to and from parties, I'd see a young married couple out walking together, and even I would be captivated by the sight of them. I guess women so long to be married that they'll stake everything on that one word. Tsukiko liked to quibble with words; maybe that's why she was so attracted by the word *married*.

Tsukiko's father had already extended her contract twice. "If he keeps this up," she wailed, "when will I ever be able to go free?" But if someone were to buy out her contract and marry her, she'd be free.

Tsukiko said that her elder sister had been sold to the Shibata Circus.[2] And then, at first, her father had taken Tsukiko to the circus, meaning to sell her too. But her elder sister had pleaded with him in tears: do anything, but please, don't sell her to the circus.

Well, if the circus was that bad, he decided, he'd sell her to a geisha house instead. "The circus would've been better," Tsukiko always said. "So long as you do your act, you don't have to do it with *danna*."

Tsukiko seemed to find sleeping with *danna* the most painful thing of all. On mornings after she'd spent the night with someone, she'd jump into the bath as soon as she got back and scrub her whole body with soap so many times it was as if she were trying to cleanse her very veins.

"Don't be silly, Tsukiko!" I'd laugh. "You can't wash out your insides, you know!"

"If I could pull them out, I would," Tsukiko would say tearfully. "That's how much I'd like to wash out my insides! Ugh, it's disgusting! Just disgusting!"

Once I thought I'd show Tsukiko my "secret place," and we set off in the middle of the night. I'd taken her there especially to show her the beautiful night vista, but she just couldn't get up the tree. "Climb!" I told her. I got annoyed and tried to push her from below. "No, it's too scary," she said, and just wouldn't budge. I was cross and sulked.

"Elder Sister, forgive me! I'll wait down here," she said, hugging my wooden sandals and sitting on a rock. Ever since Karuta had gone away, I'd been closest to Tsukiko. For her part, Tsukiko thought of me as the only person she could talk to and in many ways depended on me.

Then without any warning, Tsukiko killed herself. Elder Sister Sennari read me her farewell note.

Elder Sister Crane, Hii-san's dumped me. I was going to have a baby and so I told Hii-san. But he insulted me. "You, a geisha, are trying to tell me you're going to have my baby? That's a line some nice girl might use. But how can a woman who does it for money tell anybody she's going to have his child?" Elder Sister, please believe me. The child I'm carrying is Hii-san's. I'm going to die to prove it. Please, tell Hii-san for me.

I was so shocked I felt as if my heart had been smashed to smithereens.

Mother screeched and yelled, looking as if she were about to beat up the girl's dead body. "That shameless ingrate! Who the hell does she think she's been living on all these years? I've spent more than 300 yen on that bitch!"

This was more than I could bear. "Mother! She's dead now! Please, leave her in peace. Couldn't you at least say, 'poor thing'?"

She turned on all of us. "Poor thing! I'm the one who's the poor thing! She's run out on her debts! And it's going to cost money to clear up this mess besides!" Mother looked a perfect demon of greed; so much so that I glanced back, half expecting to see her mouth split wide open to the ears. On the night of the wake, she was still complaining to those who had come to pay their respects. I couldn't bear to be anywhere near her, so I slipped out of the house and went down to the shores of Lake Suwa. I thought I might shed a tear for Tsukiko there, but all I could do—for no particular reason, to no one in particular—was to mutter "Beast! Beast!"

It was heartrending. Why was Tsukiko ever born? It was too awful. "You're no Miss Nice Girl." What on earth is that supposed to mean? Does he mean to say that geisha aren't human beings? Cut a geisha and she hurts; red blood comes out. We're not cold-blooded creatures. Does he think we're geisha because we want to be? That we just love doing it? Everybody wants the blessing of being a bride one day. So how is it that Tsukiko and I are geisha? If you have no father, you're despised; if you're a geisha, they call you unclean. Who decides that's the way it should be? No matter how I looked at it, it just wasn't fair.

That horrid old demon, that hag! That no-faced queer bastard Hii! I'll get back at you, mark my word! If someone is injured, the assailant is punished under the law. But a person can be killed without anyone ever lifting a finger; and the killer isn't punished at all. Could anything be more unfair? If you push a person that far, you should be given a taste of your own medicine.

Tsukiko's suicide was a turning point for me; after that, I was a changed person. No longer could I go on as I had before, doing just as I was told, trying my best to keep in everyone's good graces. Or was it rather that until then I'd known nothing of the world and had just been groping in the dark?

I made up my mind. There was no reason why we should be the only ones who were humiliated, why we should never resist. Until then, my situation had never seemed strange to me, but now I resented with all my heart being a geisha; I hated this world. On this planet called Earth, people build things called houses, of which men say, "This one's mine, that one's mine," fighting among one another to possess as much as they possibly can, crying and laughing all the while. Well, this is a world, I made up my mind, we'd be better off without.

REVENGE

Hii-san, the man who'd killed Tsukiko, was the son of the owner of a small factory in Suwa. It used to be a small silk mill, but they had converted it into a munitions plant and were doing rather well as a result.[3] Hii-san suffered from consumption or something, they said, and was very pale. He played around a lot and fancied himself a great connoisseur of women. War had turned the filthy beggar into a rich boy!

On the fifth day after Tsukiko's death, I ran into him in the corridor of a restaurant. "Oh Hii-san," I said, gazing at him adoringly. "I haven't seen you for ages! There's something I just have to tell you."

"Miss Crane? To me? Surely you must be mistaken!"

"No, you're the one I want to talk to. Please, just this once!" I hurried away. What a fool! Did he really think I'd cozy up to him without something particular in mind? After that, whenever I saw him I'd turn on the charm; when I was called to one of Hii-san's parties, I'd pour saké and exchange cups with him, working all my wiles and deceptions on him for two hours or more; then at the last minute, I'd escape. They say that there's a knack to catching fish; well, there's a knack to catching men, too.

On the fishing analogy, then, I was the fish and Hii-san was the fisherman, and the fish was trying to get herself caught. I'm yours for the catching, I let him think, and then escape with the bait five or six times. By which time, the amount he'd spent on bait had begun to build up and he'd become more and more determined to catch me the next time. With this trick, bit by bit, I got him hooked.

This one didn't seem to like the coolly elegant geisha type. I'd once heard some talk of Hugo and Rodin, so I just repeated what I'd heard. He was delighted. "What an intellectual you are!" he said. As he became more and more serious about me, I could almost feel my hands closing around him. I knew I had him.

Then one day, toward the end of my eighteenth year, I was summoned to a restaurant in the middle of the day. "It's from Hii-san, and you're to wear everyday kimono." Today's the day, I thought; now I'm going to do what I've been longing to do so long. I dressed as demurely and neatly as I could, not letting a hint of geisha show. For thirty minutes I chatted with him, bowing my head sweetly and keeping my hands clasped. Somehow I sensed that the moment was drawing close, and just then Hii-san drew himself up and broached the subject.

"For the longest time I've been wanting to ask you this, but— will you marry me?"

So you've said it! The hours I've endured with you and that horrid icy feeling you give me, just to make you say that! I smiled inwardly.

"Do I look so desperate, Hii-san, that I'd be glad to have you ask me to marry you?"

If he says that, I'll say this, and if he says this, I'll say that—I'd wracked my brain (what little I have, at any rate); I'd studied long and hard to come up with those words.

"Hey! Quit laughing at me! I'm serious, you know. Don't you like me?"

"It's not a matter of like or dislike. I do this for money. I'm for sale; you're the buyer. Unfortunately there's no way I can put it more delicately in words that would meet with the approval of such a fine gentleman as yourself."

"What are you talking about? I love you, Little Crane!"

"Oh don't give me that! I'm no Miss Nice Girl. If you want to catch a geisha, you don't have to tell her you love her, you know. Don't talk such nonsense, please." I got up to leave, but Hii-san grabbed my hands and tried to pull me back down, determined, apparently, to make me see things his way.

"You mean to force me into it, then? Shall I spread it around the quarter that the great Hii-san has forced me to marry him? It'd do my reputation a world of good! For your information, I've never spent time with you because I like you. If you thought I did, that's a credit to my long years of business experience. Too bad, isn't it? We had fun together as customer and geisha. But I haven't sunk so low that I have to accept the favor of your marrying me!"

He was crushed. "Don't you understand when a man's being sincere?"

"Sincere you say? Do you think you can kill anyone you like with that word? I don't happen to have the courage to commit suicide."

"So it's Tsukiko you're on about, is it? I can't stand gloomy women. I've always been looking for a little bird who can sing me a happy song. If you want to be loved, you'd better make an effort. Women who don't make an effort, who don't get on with things, they're like birds that don't sing."

"But no matter how much you want to sing, if you're fed bad food you can't, right? Marriage, love, sincerity, are those the only tricks you've got up your sleeve? If you think that all geisha are going to sob tears of gratitude and fall down on their knees when they hear those words, you're very much mistaken. That's infantile, that's what it is. I know much more exciting words than those."

I looked down in disgust on that dumbfounded and dumbstruck man, then, raising a cry of victory, marched home.

Chapter 5 🦋 Awakening to Love

NUMBER TWO AND NUMBER THREE

As the end of 1943 approached, there was talk of the new clothes we'd need for the New Year's celebrations. When I mentioned this to Cockeye, he said it would be a waste to spend money on clothes of that sort, since I was going to quit work as a geisha anyhow. The year's delay that he'd agreed to with Mother was up, and before long Cockeye would be buying me out.

For a geisha, to have your contract redeemed and become a mistress is a giant step up in the world. Living "with a cat in your lap and a fan in your hand," as we put it, was everyone's fondest hope. But for some reason I found it depressing.

In the end, though, there was nothing that someone in my position could do about it, no matter who the buyer might be. Either way, there was a rope around your neck; what difference did it make who held the other end of it? I had no way of knowing how much money changed hands between Cockeye and Mother at the Takenoya.

Cockeye bought me a two-story house by the lakeshore, and I moved there just after the new year. I was Cockeye's Number Three, his second mistress, but he told me he'd introduce me to Number Two.[1] Full of curiosity, I went with him one day to meet her. Number Two ran a restaurant in the town of Lower Suwa.

She was fresh and beautiful, reminiscent of bright yellow *nanohana* blossoms; that was my first impression of her. "I've heard so much about you," she said. "I've wanted very much to meet you." She smiled serenely, without a trace of antagonism on her face.

I'd heard that she was beautiful but never imagined I'd find her so impeccable. If she had said something hostile, I was going to say, "You came first; I came later. He got sick of you, so he turned to me. You're the one who's to blame." But this little speech I'd prepared turned out to be unnecessary, and I felt a bit deflated.

When Cockeye left the room, she said, "I must tell you how grateful I am. Thanks to you, I'll be free of him a great deal more than I used to be."

I sensed no hint of resentment in her words; she was open and straightforward. Completely won over, I blurted out my own true feelings.

"You mean you don't like him either? Me too!" At this she lowered her head and laughed, and the reserve of our first meeting evaporated; we were in complete accord with each other. I told her I'd worked out that his nickname, "Lon-Pari," meant "One eye looking at London and the other eye looking at Paris." Number Two squeezed my arm and laughed. Perhaps it was the shared misery of being kept women that made us feel this way, but without ever mentioning it, we both knew that we could tell each other things without endangering our positions.

From then on I often went to visit her on my own. Number Two was a great talker, and I always ended up staying longer than I'd intended. I really meant it when I said to her once, "Maybe I should come and live with you?"

"You mustn't think like that!" she said. "That man's a monstrous weirdo. If you don't coax something substantial for yourself out of him now, you'll be in big trouble when you end up in my position. The house and the land are in my name, so I can support myself without too much difficulty. But if you don't have anything, and then he changes his mind about you, you'll be destitute. Men are greedy. If you get him to spend money on you now, he won't want what he's spent to go to waste, and he'll spend more; then you'll never have to worry about being abandoned."

"But you're the jewel in his collection," she went on. "I'm sure you have nothing to worry about. When I think of all you sweet young things, I feel quite miserable."

Even at my age I was no stranger to the art of manipulating men, but Number Two was thirty-four or thirty-five, and I was only nineteen; to her I must have seemed very green.

"Elder Sister, even I know a trick or two, you know."

"Do you now? A great trickster, are you?"

We laughed happily about things like this, and then we'd go our separate ways; but Number Two taught me all sorts of techniques for extracting a bit more from the monster.

When the monster found out that I went so often to Number Two's place, he was furious. "With the two of you scheming to-gether there's no telling what you'll get up to. Naoko's a devious woman; she'll never have anything decent to say. You're not to go there again!"

"Elder Sister Naoko's beautiful and intelligent. You bought out her contract yourself, so there's nothing wrong with her. In fact, she's marvelous," I retorted, singing her praises and grinning from ear to ear. "Serves you right!" I thought, inwardly delighted. "Can't answer that one, can you?"

Tricks of the Love Trade

In the house Cockeye had bought me, I lived for a while doing nothing at all. It was lonely, though, being cooped up indoors every day, and I sometimes felt I'd like to go back to work as a geisha. But the war situation was growing desperate, and the rumor was that if you weren't doing anything useful, you could be drafted and sent away who knows where. If that was so, I put it to Cockeye, then I wanted to get a job of some sort. Cockeye knew someone high up in Nippon Wireless and quickly worked something out with him. In May I began working.

My job, if you could call it that, was in the department where they made "grids," components of radio tubes, but it was more like play than work. The materials were never available, so we couldn't do any work at all. The people in the workshop made lunch boxes; the people in the glass department spent the whole day making tumblers and foot warmers, which they assiduously carried home with them. At this rate, I thought, how are we ever going to win the war?

Before long, I noticed that the women made a point of avoiding me.

"They say she was a geisha, that one."

"They say she's someone's mistress, you know. At any rate, she's got some guy wrapped around her little finger; deceived him completely!"

Bits and pieces of malicious gossip like this began to come my way. I was plunged into a dark depression. Was I going to be dogged by the labels *geisha* and *mistress* wherever I went? Maybe I should just quit. But then I remembered how Cockeye had scoffed the day it was decided I could go to the factory. "All you know how to do is sleep in until ten in the morning and sit in front of the mirror while you fix your hair and stroke your bum! If you last a month, I'll give you the Gold Medal for Bravery in Battle!" It was frustrating, but I couldn't give up.

Then one day I made an important discovery. The son of a liquor merchant was working here. He was a second lieutenant who'd become ill and had been excused temporarily from military service; but he didn't think it fair that he should be idle while his friends were still fighting, so he'd come to work here. His name was Motoyama-san. He'd probably be returning to his unit shortly, I heard people saying, and a lot of girls would be heartbroken when he did. So these women despise me, and the men look at me with a leering curiosity. All right then, I decided; I'll make Motoyama-san mine and really put their noses out of joint.

First I had to make him aware of my existence. From that day forward I stopped smoking in front of other people and began playing the part of the dejected young lady. At lunch break I would sit all by myself someplace where he could see me. I did everything in my power to attract his attention without letting people realize it was an act. Even if I didn't have a pretty face and a graceful figure, at nineteen I still had plenty of confidence in my ability to attract the interest of a man. If he happened to glance my way, I didn't waste the opportunity but gazed back at him with an indefinably imploring look. On the way home from the factory, I'd make sure I was slightly ahead of him, head drooping, walking along despondently.

I must have looked a pitiful sight, for there were some people who spoke to me sympathetically, but I looked back at them coldly and didn't respond. My plans would be ruined if he got the mistaken impression that I was happily engaged in conversation with another man. "Small sacrifices for the greater goal," I told myself, persevering doggedly with my plan. Maybe you can't say this as a general rule, but I was convinced that most men's hearts were terribly susceptible to feelings of pity.

One morning about two months later, I heard on the weather forecast that it would rain in the afternoon, and so I went out without an umbrella. This was my chance! When the time came to go home, it was still raining. Choosing my time carefully, I set out in front of him. By the time I got to the gate, he'd run up behind me, thrust a Western-style umbrella into my hands, and rushed away. I was a bit flustered myself. All I'd wanted was to make him feel sorry for me. . . .

That night I went to the Takenoya and asked Father to write a letter for me, "something soulful and passionate, something just bound to move a man." Mother laughed at me. "You're up to some mischief again, I'll bet!" Actually there was a reason she said "again."

Just after Cockeye bought out my contract, while I was still living at the Takenoya, I ran into a young customer of mine on the street. "How about a quick one?" he said, inviting me for a drink. "Why not earn my supper while I'm at it?" Thinking nothing of it, I went along with him. As we parted, he said, "Let's meet again," and since I didn't particularly dislike him, we met for a drink two or three times after that.

Whenever I went out to meet him, I asked them at the Takenoya to tell Cockeye, if he telephoned, that, yes, I was in and then let me know immediately. But I was found out nonetheless. We'd arranged to meet, and I was just on my way out when Cockeye turned up.

"Where do you think you're going at this hour?"

"Nowhere," I replied.

"Well I know what you're up to. And I won't have you behaving like some cheap whore!" He was purposely trying to rub me the wrong way.

I was so angry that I paid 2 yen for some black-market saké, which should have cost only 90 sen, and drank it with Father. I decided not to go out for the time being. Father laughed, "It's all your own fault, you know!" But I didn't think I'd done anything wrong.

Anyway, the letter for Motoyama-san was ready. It said something like this:

> I've never once been treated kindly by people in my whole life—
> your kindness brought tears to my eyes. Everyone scorns me be-
> cause I was a geisha. But what have I ever done to anyone? If there
> is something bad about me, please be so good as to let me know.

The next day I'd hand it to him, careful not to let anyone see me, and wait for his reaction.

THE WITCHER BEWITCHED

The letter was most effective. The day after I'd given it to him, he responded with a friendly letter. "I've done it!" I thought, smiling with satisfaction. Once I'd got this far, the rest was easy. We exchanged two or three more letters, and in my last letter I had them write this for me:

> That I've been able to meet such a kind person as yourself must
> surely be the work of the gods. Once, just once, would be
> enough. I'd like to talk to you. If I am to be punished, humble
> creature that I am, for daring to have such a desire, I would, with
> no regrets, give the rest of my life for the chance to talk with you
> alone just once. Whatever punishment the heavens may send, I
> accept it willingly. I shall wait for you at the lakeside from eight
> o'clock this evening until dawn.

At long last I got my wish. I succeeded in meeting him by the lake. "I feel so very sorry for you," he said passionately. "I'll do anything in my power to brighten your lonely smile. People mustn't ever grovel. Come what may, you've got to stand proud, plant both feet firmly on the ground, and stride forward."

"What a lot of nonsense!" I thought, proud and arrogant in my success. "Say what you like, all men are the same. You're just another man, and I'm using you as a tool for my own ends. You seem to think I'm just an ordinary woman, but I'm the mistress of a monster. I'm a witch!" Such were my reckless thoughts; but to him I said sadly, "I've been badly used since I was a child. I haven't the courage to rebel, and I wouldn't know how to, either."

Until we could meet again, I stayed away from the factory, because I figured it would be more effective to make him wonder what had become of me. When we met on the appointed day, I told him, "There's something I simply must show you!" and dragged him off to a restaurant.

"This is the only thing I know how to do." I played the shamisen and danced until he forgot how much time had passed, and I plied him with saké until he lost all self-control. He was astonished and dumbfounded when I threw myself into his arms. "You don't have to . . ." he said, flustered, but I pulled him into the next room, where I'd already arranged the bedding. "I like you so very much," I whispered, snatching a quick glance to gauge his expression.

He made passionate love to me. Later, when he was himself again, he sat up on the mattress and, without warning, began to sob his apologies. This wasn't what I had in mind! I was completely nonplussed.

"If only I didn't have to go back into the army, I'd marry you, right now! But I've already dedicated my life to our country. I don't know when I might die, so I mustn't do anything irresponsible." It was all he could do to get the words out, he was so overcome.

"I'm not asking for anything. What's responsibility got to do with liking someone? All I know is that I like you very much."

"What can I do to make you happy? It was wrong of me, forgive me. But while I'm still here, let's meet every night. If only I could make it up to you, I'd ask for another life." Even I began to understand what it meant to say that someone was entirely in earnest.

After that, even when we were at the factory, he looked after me, heedless of what other people might think; and on the way home, he walked with me. My previous experience had been only of men who would whisper their burning desire for you when no one could see them and pretend they didn't know you when others were around.

I felt that for the first time I knew the happiness of being loved, not as a geisha, but as a woman. Even though, thinking back, I'd approached him only to have my revenge on everyone who had looked askance at me. I never for the life of me imagined that I'd be treated with such respect. In my lonely heart, a faint glimmer of love had been kindled, and I began to feel that I must do everything in my power not to extinguish it.

True love

At the factory, our eyes would have only to meet, and I'd feel my whole body bathed in the warmth of his love. We waited for each other by the shores of the lake every evening between seven and eight o'clock. As he gazed at the lights of the town reflected on the surface of the water, he would tell me beautiful legends about the stars in the sky or the stories of *Little Lord Fauntleroy* and *A Little Princess*.[2] He taught me, too, about the "morality" that's supposed to exist in human society. He explained to me why "misfortune may turn out to be a blessing in disguise" and how if we could just trust in fate, like the old man in the story, we'd never suffer the pangs of worry and anguish.[3]

"Before I got to know you, I tried to live like that. But when I think about your future happiness, I do worry. If I were to tell my parents about you now and ask their understanding, I'm sure they'd let us get married. But after I go back to the front, it would just mean more suffering for you, since you have so little experience of the world. It'd make you more unhappy than you are now. But if that's what you want to do, it's all right by me, though . . ."

What an absurd idea! He wasn't to know, but there was a rope around my neck, and Cockeye held the other end. Yet if only I were free, how I'd love to be called his wife, I thought to myself, even if only for three days!

From the day I'd been born up until that moment, I had learned only two things: the geisha arts and how to sleep with men. I knew nothing except how to be sexy. So when we'd meet, I'd suggest, perhaps one time in three, "Shall we go to an inn?" As far as relationships between men and women were concerned, I thought that was all there was; I couldn't imagine anything else. But he would remonstrate with me earnestly, "You shouldn't say things like that!" He treated me with such respect that it was torture.

Cockeye came over once every three days. Even when I was with him, during the hour between seven and eight o'clock, my thoughts would fly to the lakeside, and I'd grow moody and irritable. When the eight o'clock chimes would ring, I'd try my best to forget about it, but the feeling of dissatisfaction and loneliness would linger.

"Do you love me?" I asked Cockeye one day.

"What idiot would spend such huge sums of money to get someone he didn't think was cute?"

"What is love, anyhow?"

"It's when you just can't be satisfied until something's all yours."

"But isn't it when you hope the other person'll be happy?"

"Well, isn't that why I bought you your freedom?" he said, pleased with himself.

It was hopeless. There was no way I could make him understand. One slip of the tongue and he'd be on to me. If Cockeye ever found out about *him*, it would all be over.

Motoyama-san taught me that "loving someone has nothing to do with your physical self; it's a spiritual longing, it's trusting each other, it's wanting the other person to be happy, it's getting outside yourself; that's what true love is."

I'd have been just as upset if Motoyama-san found out about that toad of a man as if Cockeye found out about him. I made him believe it was because I was living in someone else's house that I couldn't stay out late every night. Whenever I was with him, I was in constant terror that we'd be seen by someone I knew. The pressure was horrific; I was almost gnashing my teeth I was so tense. Unable to bear the strain, I would break down crying for no reason at all. I don't know what he made of it, but he worried constantly about me. "Don't cry! Let's try to work out how you're going to manage in the future."

I had no particular dreams or hopes for my future. All I wanted was to spend as much time as I could with him. But our secret rendezvous didn't last even a month: as the autumn winds began to blow, our trysting was brought to a halt. I had incurred the wrath of Cockeye.

Attempted suicide

Actually, it would have been strange if I hadn't been found out, since I was out of the house every evening between seven and eight o'clock. Cockeye had been sniffing around for some time, asking irksome questions on one pretext or another; but I'd managed somehow to keep him in good humor and evade the issue. But one night he just wouldn't let up.

"You've been hanging around with some punk lately, haven't you? Well I won't have you messing around like some filthy whore!"

Finally, I'd had enough. "We intend to get married."

"Suit yourself—see if I care! But before you do, I'll tell that little shit a thing or two. My face is pretty well known in these parts. If I told people I'd given you up so you could marry, it'd all sound very nice; but what if it got about that someone had been messing with my woman and stole her right out of my bed? I'd be a laughingstock. I'll knock him dead! Does he think he can piss all over me and I'll just run away and hide?" Toad that he was, moisture glistened on his bald head, and the sweat rolled off him as he raged.

I'd rather die than force *him* to listen to such abuse, I thought; but when I tried to flee, he caught me under his arm, lifted me up over his head, and whacked me down, thud, on the tatami. As I lay there weeping, I was also thinking: more than anything else, I didn't want *him* to have to see this toad; if ever it came to that, I'd stab the toad to death.

But what was the point? *He* would soon be leaving; he might never wake from his beautiful dream! I didn't want him to know now that I was someone's mistress. If he were to find out that all those sweet things I'd said with such an earnest face had all been lies, there was no telling how sad it would make him, how he'd despise me. Trembling with fear, I pressed both hands to the floor and apologized.

"I've been bad! I promise I'll never do anything to upset you, ever again! Please forgive me!"

"So you've come to your senses, have you?" said the toad, quite cheered up.

"Yes, I have. I'll never see him again," I vowed; and gritting my teeth, I went to work placating and cajoling him.

Cockeye was the sort of man who, once he got what he wanted, would fall sound asleep with his mouth wide open. His false teeth stuck out, vibrating with every breath; and although I was determined I wouldn't look at them, they forced themselves on my sleepless eyes. Disgusting! Just disgusting! I found him more loathsome that night than ever before. I lay awake until dawn, shuddering all the while with revulsion.

The next day I didn't go to the factory. I shut myself up in the house the whole day through, fairly smoldering with discontent. But when the lights began to come on in town, I couldn't suppress my desire to be with him. I sat down in front of the mirror. I picked up my shamisen. Six o'clock came and went, then seven. He must be waiting, as always, by the lakeside. I couldn't bear simply to disappear without saying anything to him. Perhaps I could go just this once, make up some excuse why I can't see him anymore, then leave him? But I knew only too well what my toad was like. He could be foolishly trusting, beating his breast and sighing, "Oh, all right then!" But make one false step and he'd be smashing my door down to get at me.

But what do I care? If he gets nasty, then that's when I stab him and kill him, and I die, too. In the end I fled the house. But this was a monster, and who could know what schemes he might have up his sleeve? I gave the old woman who used to wash the bedding at the Takenoya 1 yen and asked her to bring Motoyama-san to me; meanwhile I managed to hire a room.

"My mother's been taken ill and I've got to go home!" No sooner were the words out of my mouth than I buried my face in his chest and began to sob aloud like a child.

"What an unfortunate creature you are! If it's all right with you, I'll go with you." It was kind of him to offer, but I shook my head weakly and put him off. If only I really did have a home in the countryside, we could go there just the two of us, even if only for a day, and enjoy ourselves in peace! My breast burned with this hopeless dream.

"As soon as I get back, I'll come to the factory," I said as we parted; but I had resolved, once and for all, that I would never see him again. He had made love to me only twice, no more. I, who had known more men than I could count on both hands. I was utterly defiled. If only I'd been pure of body, and free, then no matter how I might have to suffer, I could have waited ten years, twenty years, for the day when I could be his wife. . . . There was no way I could wipe myself clean. By the time I realized that, it was too late. What a fool I was! Yet what could I have done, as ignorant as I was? Mother at the Takenoya was to blame. My real mother was to blame. I cursed the world and everyone in it; I wished I could hack myself to pieces and throw them away in the river.

After I parted with Motoyama-san, I stayed in the house and never set foot outside the door.

"You miss him so much even your face is changed, is that it?" the toad said in a rage. "Well, I've got my pride, too; not on my life am I gonna let go of you!" I was determined not to erase the touch of *his* skin from mine, though; I passed the days in a delirium of anguish, steadfastly refusing to have anything to do with the toad.

On the morning of the sixth of November, Mother from the Takenoya brought around a letter from *him* and read it to me. He wrote that he'd be leaving on the fifth, on the night train, and he enclosed some money in case I needed it for anything.

That he would be leaving sometime, I knew; but I'd hoped to see him one last time before he left. The thought brought forth such a flood of tears it was as if a dam had burst. There was no point in continuing to live. I couldn't bear the torture of spending the rest of my life with that repulsive Cockeye. And even if I should try, it would be a life with nothing to look forward to. I decided finally that I'd rather die while *he* still stood on Japanese soil. Choosing a day when Cockeye wouldn't be coming, I put the house in order.

By the middle of November, the Shinshū region is already quite cold, but I put on my pale pink cotton kimono with a pattern of morning glories, the one that *he* always said suited me best. I made myself up carefully and waited until it was late. As I lit a stick of incense and watched it burn away, I felt refreshed and calm. It had been twenty years of nothing but pain, but at long last I, too, would find peace.

At eleven o'clock I shut the door and stepped outside. A sliver of moon hung in the cold night sky, Lake Suwa brimmed with water, and as always the lights of the town twinkled beautifully. Everything brought back memories of him. Calling out to a vision of him, I threw myself in.

Death by drowning is painful. The water roars as it beats against your eardrums; the water stings your nose as it penetrates to the top of your brain. For a time I gulped it down; then I lost consciousness.

Some time later, to my surprise, I awoke in a hospital room. They told me I'd been rescued by someone who'd gone out to do a bit of night fishing. I couldn't bring myself to say thank you to the person who'd saved me. Didn't he understand that I'd wanted to be at peace? I resented him bitterly. To want to die is easy; but actually to do it requires more courage than people think. And just when I'd finally dared to do it . . .

Waiting for me when I got out of hospital was Cockeye's rejection and the cold disdain of everyone else.

Chapter 6 🦋 Wanderings of a Castaway

No place to call home

"If I disgust you so much, then get out!" Cockeye told me.

"Well, if that means I can be free . . ." I said to myself; and with no thought for the future, I quite cheerfully let him turn me out without a single sen. I went straight back to the Takenoya.

But at the Takenoya, Mother pulled me up short.

"It's bad for our reputation. We can't have you back here."

All the restaurants had been closed down by government order, so I had no place to go and no idea what to do.[1] I realized then that I knew nothing about any place other than this "flower-and-willow" district. I was at my wit's end. Well then, I would go and see the mistress of the Ichiriki; she had always been good to me. To the Ichirikiya I went.

"I'm under strict instructions to do nothing for you," she said. "I'm terribly sorry, but that's the way it is." The mistress of the Ichiriki gave me 5 yen, warning me that she would be in big trouble if I told anyone.

Taking the money, I spent the night at an inn, but I was so worried I couldn't sleep a wink. I knew now that here in Suwa, with Cockeye breathing heavily down everyone's neck, there was no longer any place I could call home. There was no doubt about it; he had threatened everyone. I suppose this was his scheme to make life difficult for me so I'd feel grateful to him. Were I tamely to return to him, I'd be bound by a rope ten times thicker than before; I'd be Cockeye's slave for the rest of my life. It would be absolutely unbearable. Yet I didn't have the courage to throw myself into the lake again. I was cornered.

And that's when I thought of my mother. When my uncle had taken me away from that landlord's house, we had trudged along until we reached my mother's home. And her cold gaze. But she was my mother, she had given birth to me; surely she would do something for me. With these thoughts in mind, I decided I would go to her.

The next morning I went by train to Shiojiri, and with only my memory to guide me, I eventually found the house, but the mother I had counted on was not there. People said that when her husband died six years ago, she had farmed out the four children separately and gone off somewhere with another man. One of my younger brothers was living nearby at a plasterer's, I heard. Straightaway I went to find him.

A child burned black by the sun and dressed in rags turned out to be my little brother. He stared at me wide-eyed.

"Do you remember me?"

"Nope."

"Do you know where Ma's gone?"

"Nope."

With tears in his eyes, he answered me brusquely. I had him tell me where Uncle's house was, and then I trudged off again, clutching at my empty stomach. Last night's accommodation was 4 yen and the train fare was 25 sen, so I had only 75 sen in my pocket. Worse still, it was getting dark, and I couldn't find the house I was searching for. I had never felt so forlorn. Dear Motoyama-san! If only he were with me, he would help me. At some point my thoughts had turned to him.

A BROTHER'S LOVE

Eventually I found Uncle's house, and what a pitiful sight it was! The walls were crumbling, and you could see right into it.

"Beg pardon!" I called out. My aunt poked her head out through a hole in the wall. Finally, when I managed to get inside and speak to her, she told me that the house had been demolished in a typhoon two years ago; my uncle had been crushed under one of the beams and died. Aunt's face was haggard with exhaustion.

"If a body can just keep her belly full, she's pretty well off, I reckon."

As she spoke, she buried something that looked like a rice cake in the ashes of the hearth.

With no shame or concern for what she might think, I made a clean breast of everything that had happened to me.

"Please put me up for a bit," I begged her.

The house had been completely destroyed in the typhoon, and she lived in a hut, of only one room at that.

"In any case, just let me lie down," I said, utterly exhausted.

Crawling beneath the rag that passed for a quilt, I tried to sleep but I was so worn out, I guess, that I was unable to drop off. Even after my aunt had fallen asleep, I lay awake, helpless to do anything but weep, thinking about what was to become of me, longing for *him*.

Then I sensed that someone was outside. Between where I lay and outside, there was not a wooden door but only a single paper panel. I slid it open quietly. Lo and behold, there stood my little brother, whom I supposed I'd already left behind.

"What on earth are you doing here at this hour?" I asked him.

"I hate it at the plasterer's," he said, sobbing.

There was nothing I could do but to let him into the house, and when I asked him what had happened, he said he'd followed me here secretly.

"If it's so awful, you don't have to go back. I'll think of something."

I still had a hopelessly optimistic idea of what life in this world was like. The next day I begged my aunt to put him up as well as me.

"I'll earn the boy's keep and pay you, OK?"

I had her take me to the sawmill where she worked and got them to give me a job. But by the evening of my first day of work, I was so exhausted I felt as if the bones of my arms and legs had been pulverized. Here was a life that until now I could never have imagined.

For lunch they ate boiled sweet potatoes, but with no salt to put on them. For the evening meal they had what they called "grilled rice cake" (*yakimochi*), but not even the white sort, made of wheat flour, that you get in town; they were just balls of flour made from barley that had been milled, hulls and all. They roasted them in the hearth, tapping and blowing off the ashes as they ate.

Until just three days ago, at Cockeye's house, I'd had nothing but good food to eat. "Carp tastes muddy, I can't eat it; smelt is too fishy, I can't eat it," I would say. I was dreadfully spoiled and had picked up all sorts of bad habits. But no matter how hungry I was, I couldn't get these "rice cakes" down my throat.

My aunt would call it a first-class treat when she would serve us round slices of white radish; but again there was no salt or soy sauce, and so they were steeped in the dregs of vinegar from a empty jar of pickled plums.

The people who worked at the sawmill brought "grilled rice cakes" and pumpkin in their lunch boxes. As they ate, they would say, "Even if you do happen to get a bit of rationed rice, there's no salt, no *miso* [bean paste]. If there's *miso*, not only do you get no rice, there aren't even any sweet potatoes. How I'd love to fill my belly with white rice and *miso* soup." "The old folks at home say that just once before they die, they'd like to eat a bowl of white rice big enough to stand their chopsticks up in without their falling over." To me this was utterly astonishing.

Physically I was in a pitiful state. My joints ached horribly; if I was standing, I had to sit; if I was sitting, I had to stand up. Although I was dizzy and near collapse, I went to work doing the job that my aunt did. I couldn't get anything down my throat, and so by the morning of the third day, I was unable even to get up. I took the day off. I felt like I must have a high fever, too. As I lay there, drifting in and out of consciousness, my little brother woke me.

"Here, eat this." Gingerly he pushed a bowl of white rice porridge toward the bed. Recalling how my aunt had complained the previous evening that there wasn't a grain of rice to be had, I asked him, "How did you get this?"

"When I lived with Ma, there was never any rice, so when I was at the plasterer's, I used to take a little bit every day when I washed the rice, thinking that I'd give it to her when she got back. You don't eat anything, and it'd be terrible if you died; so yesterday I secretly brought it here and boiled it up," my brother said, his eyes welling with tears.

When I thought how this child, just thirteen years old, hands raw from chilblains, had washed and cooked the rice every day, with no resentment for the mother who had abandoned him, I marveled at the sweetness of his nature and swallowed my tears.

The next day my brother did not appear, even when it got dark. What was he up to? I wondered. Had he perhaps got fed up and gone back to the plasterer's? Late in the evening he returned, and thrusting something toward me, he said, "Here, drink this."

"What is it?" I asked, hesitating.

"Tea brewed from dried earthworms," he replied.

If you hold a broken pane of glass against the surface of the water and look through it, apparently you can see the bottom of the river clearly. Even though it was midwinter and freezing cold, he had spent half the day fishing bits of scrap metal out of the river in this way. Then he'd sold them for 2 sen and bought the dried earthworms, with which he'd made the tea. Besides this, since there was nothing to be found in the nearby river, he'd gone to the river in town, and that was why he was so late, he said.

He crawled under the foot of my quilt, and as he lay curled up there, I felt how cold his feet were, and I thought that no matter what it took, even if I had to slice off bits of my own flesh and sell them, I would make him happy. I was that determined. The sight of my little brother, starved for familial affection and desperate that I should not die and leave him, was etched painfully in my heart.

Another time, on a rainy day, he picked up cigarettes for me. "How I'd love a smoke!" I was always sighing, and so he went more than a mile to the next town and picked up three or four cigarette butts. Wet from the rain, yellowed and torn, he carried them back in hands that were numb with cold and silently presented them to me.

TEARS OF HUMILIATION

If I was to make a decent life for my little brother, there was no point in staying in a place like this, so I decided I would go to Elder Sister Karuta in Chiba. But when I talked it over with my aunt, she said that there was no money for the train fare.

She saw there was no way she could change my mind, and so eventually she managed to scrape together 50 sen for me, and we went first to Upper Suwa. I had my brother wait by the shore of the lake, where Motoyama-san and I always used to meet, while I ran to the Ichiriki.

"Please!" I said to the mistress of the Ichiriki, "Lend me 10 yen!"

"Business is bad these days," she said. Then she thought. "What about asking Hii-san? He was infatuated with you, remember?" She meant the Hii-san who had killed Tsukiko. Clenching my teeth, I nodded. For my little brother, I would endure any humiliation whatever.

There was no rice, no *miso*, and all the restaurants were closed; but this world still had its hidden underside. Eventually Hii-san turned up, in one of the party rooms at the Ichiriki.

"Surely there must be some mistake," he sneered sarcastically.

I kept a grip on myself and started talking. "Please, buy me for the night for 10 yen."

"The peerless Miss Crane for 10 yen? That's dirt cheap! You think I'd pass that up? But in return, you know, you're mine; you're prepared for anything, right?" As he spoke, his mouth twisted in a savage smile. I looked straight into the man's eyes and egged him on.

"Whatever you wish."

"I'm not so hard up for women that I'm reduced to sleeping with someone who's lost her looks. I'll buy you because I want to see you dance naked. All right? Otherwise forget it." Hii-san stared at me coldly.

Without a word I stripped off my kimono, spread it out, and knelt down on it. The man began clapping time with his hands and nodded for me to begin. I obeyed. So determined was I not to cry that I bit my lips until I drew blood—and began dancing like a madwoman. Even the ugly scar on my leg was exposed.

"Well now, come have a drink," he said, guffawing scornfully. When I took the cup of saké that he passed me, my hands were trembling.

That should do it, I thought; but as I reached silently for my kimono, the man lunged at me like a wild animal. Without resisting or reacting in any way, I lay down. Feeling the tears stream down my cheeks, I thought of my little brother who would be waiting for me, shivering with cold.

WAR'S END

I left the Ichiriki, met my brother, and that evening we set out for Chiba on the 8:05 Shinjuku train. I remembered the address from her second letter; we asked at the police box and found our way there.

Elder Sister welcomed us as warmly as if we were her own flesh and blood.

"You can't possibly take care of your brother all by yourself," her *danna* said. "I know this man, he's a bit old, but . . ." And he arranged for me to became the mistress of a sixty-three-year-old man who would look after both of us. Somehow we managed, at least without wanting for food. The man ran a small fishing business in the village of Goi, near the city of Ichihara in Chiba Prefecture, and only rarely visited the room we rented in Karuta's house, so we lived a comparatively carefree life.

But just when we had settled in, the house was burned down in the firebomb raid on the night of August 7, and we were left with nothing. We were collecting sheets of charred galvanized iron and had just begun to build a shack for ourselves when the war came to an end.

I hadn't really experienced the war in any direct way, and so I didn't understand clearly what it meant for the war to end. But if this was what war was like, I thought, why couldn't it have ended a week earlier? Then our house wouldn't have burned down.

Elder Sister Karuta asked us to come along with her to Goi. Her *danna* was going to build a house for her there; we all could live in it together, she said. But I didn't want to burden her any longer, so I got the old man to buy the burned-out remains of her house, and we began our life in the shack.

I put my brother in school, keeping him back a grade, and to supplement our income, I began selling newspapers morning and evening next to the Bank of Chiba. Somehow or other we managed, but then the next year, in May 1946, the old man died of heart failure.[2]

After that, I did literally anything. In those chaotic days immediately after the war, my brother and I simply couldn't eat on what little money we had.

At first I worked in Inage at a factory making portable kitchen braziers. These braziers are molded in two halves. You put the clay into the molds, shape the inner surface with the palm of your hand, put the two halves together, and fire them. My job was to pack the clay in and shape it. It made the skin on my hands peel off, and they became quite raw; and worse, the pay was only 35 yen a month, impossible to manage on, so I quit. Even back then, it cost 10 yen to buy three mackerel.

Then an acquaintance of Karuta opened a small restaurant next door to the prefectural office, and it was arranged that I'd work there. I had two proposals of marriage during that time.

The first was from a watchmaker named Mr. Kuwano who came to eat his lunch there every day. I ran into him daily on my way home from work. At first I thought it was by accident, but as time went by I realized that he was lying in wait for me.

"Hello there! On your way home?" Mr. Kuwano would greet me, a bit shyly. As we got to know each other better, he began to ask me if I wouldn't visit him at his home, but I declined.

"I've got a younger brother; I spend my days off with him. It's very kind of you, but . . ."

"In that case, do bring your brother along, too."

He urged me so eagerly that I concluded nothing could be better if all it entailed was the two of us going over for a meal. When he asked me for the umpteenth time, I decided to accept. We ended up eating there every day I had off.

One day we arrived at Mr. Kuwano's place as usual only to find his mother there. We hadn't met before, but it seemed to me that nothing she said made much sense.

"My son was quite insistent about wanting me to meet you. . . . Pardon me for asking, but which school did you graduate from? These days even women ought to be able to read at least the local community circulars, don't you think? My son Masaharu is a bit of an odd fellow, living here all by himself, but actually we have a well-known shop in Tokyo. My daughter is a very accomplished dressmaker and has even been asked to sew garments for members of the Imperial Family. If you accept our proposal, we'll have to ask you to adapt to the ways of our family. I trust you understand that?"

She rattled on in this vein just as if I were his fiancée. I became flustered and fled as fast as I could. "You old shitbag! I used to be a geisha, I graduated from geisha school. I was a mistress, too." How good it would have felt to tell her this, all the while puffing on a cigarette. It's a pity I couldn't control my anger.

"Damn it! I'll never go there again!" I was still angry after we arrived home. But my brother was genuinely disappointed.

"Why did you run off like that? Won't we ever go again? When we got to eat such good things? That's a waste!"

When next I met Mr. Kuwano, I turned him down.

"How rude you are! I couldn't believe my ears when your mother started going on like that. Well I'll at least tell you that I've absolutely no intention of marrying."

He looked deeply pained. I was sorry I'd behaved so badly. It would have been better if I'd never gone to his place; then he wouldn't have got his hopes up and he wouldn't have had his feelings hurt, either. When he started to apologize, I shouted arrogantly, "Don't be so pathetic, a real man doesn't make excuses!" and ran off. But in my heart I was thanking him. "I know you meant well," I thought. "Please forgive me."

THE DUMPLING-SOUP DINER

The restaurant where I worked was called the "Meat-from-the-Earth Diner." We made a kind of dumpling soup from the remains of sweet potatoes after the starch had been extracted. A bowl sold for 50 sen. We opened the doors at twelve noon and closed at four, but some people used to come and buy whole potfuls, which meant that we usually sold out by two o'clock. I worked from eight until five and had three days off a month.

Everyone there was kind, but I was careful not to let slip anything about my past. I was afraid that if people found out I had been a geisha and someone's mistress, I would be despised and humiliated. I didn't take a packed lunch, not only because it was so close to home, but also because I didn't dare smoke in front of others, and I wanted to enjoy a quiet cigarette at home during my lunch break.

The owner of the diner was a greathearted fellow. He appeared to be on good terms with someone named Yamamura Shinjirō, who later became a member of the House of Representatives; I often saw them together.[3]

It was announced that the switch to the new yen would be made in February, and so my boss assiduously collected all the 50-sen coins and 1-yen notes, put them in an apple carton, and carried them home every day. At the restaurant we were told to ask customers to pay in the smallest denominations possible because we were short of change.[4]

In April the first postwar election was held, and women, too, were permitted to vote. The first characters I ever wrote were the nine syllables "Ya-ma-mu-ra Shi-n-ji-ro-o." I had my brother teach me, and chewing all the while on the pencil, I put my whole heart into memorizing them.

"I heard it from the teachers," my brother told me. "They say it's no good if you make even a single mistake. They say that even when you send a letter to someone, it's better not to try to write Chinese characters you don't know, that even with Japanese script, you make a better impression if you write clearly and correctly."

I was startled. "Surely you haven't told the teachers that your older sister can't read?"

"I'll never tell, I promise. I'd never tell anyone anything that would cause trouble for you."

My brother was a very bright boy, honest and kind. I suppose I'm partial because I'm his older sister, but I don't think I've ever met a boy as talented as he was.

This Mr. Yamamura, the man I'd I voted for, had come through once before with the Food Distribution Authority, and my boss at the restaurant told me to take them some dumpling soup. When I got there, I found four or five immaculately dressed people. "No way are such fine folk as these going to eat dumpling soup!" I thought. But I couldn't very well take the soup back without saying something, so I set it down before them and said, "You won't want to eat this, will you?" I stood there flushed with embarrassment, convinced they'd never dream of eating such stuff.

"No, no! I'd be delighted. Well then, if you'll excuse me . . ." he said, picking up the chopsticks. I was dumbfounded, but he smiled at me and said, "I make a point of accepting whatever kindnesses people show me." I felt he'd rescued me from an awkward situation. What a nice man, I thought; when election day comes, I'll cast my vote for him no matter what! On election day I got my brother to write out the characters on a slip of paper, which I took along and copied out.

The son of the owner of the "Meat-from-the-Earth Diner" was a pleasant young man named Kōzō. He was fond of foreign films, and the first one he took me to see was Deanna Durbin's *His Butler's Sister*.[5] I couldn't read the subtitles and I couldn't understand what they were saying, and it was excruciating having to pretend that I knew what was going on.

The second time he asked me, I was on the point of declining but thought the better of it. Why let a mere movie sour your relationship with someone you see every day? Of all the ridiculous things in the world, though, there can be nothing so stupid as a film with no dialogue. This one was called *Mayerling*, and I did think the scene at the end was beautiful, where someone dies who was called—Danielle Darrieux was it? When other people cried, I pretended to cry; and when other people laughed, I pretended to laugh; but I didn't understand any of it.

On the way home we were standing in the train when without any warning he said, "Sayo, will you marry me?"

"I'm sorry, I have a younger brother."

"I know. I like the brave way you take care of him. From now on, life's going to be tough. You're a real survivor; I admire you for that. Bring your brother along! My father's pretty much agreed, he says that even though you've got baggage, we'll manage. You don't have to give me an answer immediately. I've seen my share of hard times in the army. You've got to marry me, Sayo."

He whispered these things softly in my ear, as though he were talking about the film we'd just seen.

All that night I was in an agony of indecision. It wasn't that I didn't like Kōzō, but what if he found out that the bride he'd thought was such a brave young maiden was actually an old fox? The result was a foregone conclusion. I knew I couldn't keep up the pretense through the long years of a marriage. It was obvious that no matter how much he said he loved me and wanted me, once he knew that I'd been a geisha, that I'd been a mistress, he'd feel betrayed.

It took me until dawn to reach a decision. If I were to be scorned and reviled and made to cry, then I'd better do my crying right now and get it over with. My brother was the only possible excuse for refusing him. There was no other way. The next day, without saying a word, I left the restaurant.

Chapter 7   A Dream for My Little Brother

BEAUTIFUL EYES

I've just described myself, somewhat contemptuously, as an old fox; but now that I think of it, I'm stunned to realize that I was only twenty-one at the time.

My brother asked me, "Sis, why aren't you going to work?" I made a joke of it.

"Well, I've been thinking I'd become a GI whore!"[1]

He took me seriously and started crying. "Sis, if things are that bad, then I'll—I'll quit school and go to work."

My brother was everything to me. My dreams, my affections, they were all for him. He was my reason for living, the source of the courage that kept me going through bitter times. I can't count the humiliations I endured because I couldn't read or write. I wanted to educate my brother at least to the level of middle school. He needn't have a grand-sounding title or get rich and drive around in his own car. If he were to become that sort of a man—buying geisha, getting blind drunk, behaving barbarically, making people cry—what would be the point? I just wanted to make him into the sort of human being who could write his own name wherever he went, who worked honestly and didn't lack for three meals a day; someone who could walk down the main street holding his head high and swinging his arms with pride; someone who need never humble himself, no matter what the circumstances. That was all I asked. My life was already over; it was enough that I should be the soil from which he could grow. That I knew for sure.

When my brother was taken in by the plasterer, it was on the condition that they'd at least put him through primary school; but he'd been able to attend for only about half of every year and had fallen behind. This was why, when we first came to Chiba, my brother had said, "I don't want to go; I don't understand anything." But with a bit of scolding and a bit of encouragement, I made him go. I went to see his teachers and explained the situation, and I asked them to help make sure my brother wasn't bullied. After that he went cheerfully, but if I were then to set foot in the red-light district and have my brother quit school on me, it would be disastrous.

If my brother hadn't objected, I might well have gone back to the foul life I'd led before. This little boy, who had no experience of filth, begged me with those beautiful eyes, which seemed to see right to the bottom of my heart, not to go to work as a geisha or a GI whore, even if we had to eat scraps and dress in rags.

"Sis, I'll go straight to bed in the evenings; I don't have to eat. Come on, hurry up and get in bed. Once you're asleep you forget you're hungry."

Having said this, he would get into bed before it was dark and lie there staring vacantly at the ceiling. We didn't have any savings, and so we soon ran out of food. Everyday I went digging for clams to make into soup; and as we sipped it, we'd say to each other, "Wouldn't it be delicious if only we had some *miso* to put in it?"

PEDDLER

Before long I heard from a neighbor that you could make money by going out to the countryside to buy food and then reselling it in town. I went to see Elder Sister Karuta in Goi to borrow some start-up money and had myself included in the group.

But at that time you couldn't just go and buy a train ticket whenever you wanted; the whole business required extraordinary effort. First you would sleep squatting on the street with your arms around your knees; in the morning you'd finally get hold of a ticket and get on the first train; then you'd go way out into the country where no one else went, looking for things, walking for miles. You'd come back loaded with rice and your arms full of sweet potatoes and drive your weary body to Asakusa and Ochanomizu, where you'd make the rounds selling the things you'd brought back. I'll never forget the price of sweet potatoes: you'd buy them for 8 yen and sell them for 12. My little brother would look after me when I came home exhausted. Sometimes it would be as late as nine or ten at night, but he'd always be waiting up with something prepared for dinner.

We couldn't afford to buy charcoal, so we grilled, or rather smoked, our mackerel over twigs of kindling; day after day, we ate steamed sweet potatoes and that smoky mackerel. Still, when I think back to that period in my life, even now I'm overwhelmed with feelings of warmth. Sleeping on the street and buying the ticket was mostly my brother's job.

There were sixteen or seventeen of us in the foraging group. Along the way we'd split up into groups of two or three and head off into the farming villages. I used to go with two middle-aged women, but they weren't used to the work and weren't making a very good go of it. They would buy only what they needed, and then I'd buy up what they didn't want, the whole lot. But one day we couldn't get our hands on more than a few pounds of sweet potatoes. "It's not enough," they said, "but it looks like today's just a bad day; we'll go back now." It would have been unbearably lonely being left there all by myself, so I went back to the station with them, almost in tears. The pain my brother had endured, sleeping all night on the street, the train fare that had wiped out what little money we had—now it would all be wasted. But just then, as luck would have it, one of our group, Yasu-san, spoke to me.

"What's wrong? Your rucksack's empty!"

"It was a bad day today." I was on the verge of tears.

"What a shame! And there was still stuff left over where I went. . . . Go on back there and buy it!"

The last train from Narita back to Chiba left a little after five. So long as I could catch it, I'd be all right, I thought, and off I trudged again. It was almost five miles to the place Yasu-san had told me about, and another five back to the station; all in all, I'd have to walk nearly ten miles. I'd just about had it. Then Yasu-san caught up with me and said he'd come along.

Sure enough, I managed to buy a pile of sweet potatoes. My rucksack was full and I should have left it at that; but then I bought almost twenty pounds of giant radishes, which I carried off in my arms. When I got on the train, I put the bundle of radishes on top of my rucksack and secured it to my neck. The train was packed; getting on and off was almost a battle to the death. Weighed down with baggage, pushed off balance by the crowd, I was the very last to board. Yasu-san gave me a shove, and finally I grabbed hold of a hand rail inside the carriage. Having pushed me on, there was no way Yasu-san could get through the doorway himself; he had to dash around to another door.

My feet were on the floor of the train and I clung to the rail with my hands, but bent like a bow, the rest of my body and all my baggage hung outside. The bundle of radishes on top of the rucksack slipped down and hung from my neck. I struggled desperately to work my way inside the carriage, but the people inside were pushing and shoving, and I knew that if I once let go, I'd fall out of the train. One of the station attendants spotted me.

"Let go! Let go immediately!"

As I was struggling I could hear him shouting at me. In a daze, I opened my hands and let go.

Thrown back onto the platform, I fell face up on top of the sweet potatoes. I hit my back so hard it knocked the wind out of me, and I couldn't get up again right away. The station attendant was coming toward me, jabbering incomprehensibly. I lay there ashamed and miserable, but when I lifted my head and looked up, trembling with fear, there was Yasu-san standing between me and the station attendant. He said he'd seen me fall and had jumped off himself.

That was the last train, they said; the first one in the morning would leave a little after five, and there'd be no more until then. With the help of the station attendant, we arranged to stay at an inn. At the inn, we got them to boil up some of our sweet potatoes, and we ate them together. So far so good, but then it came time to go to bed—in the same room. "Looks like more trouble!" I thought to myself.

Yasu-san began telling me the following story:

A long time ago, I was a gangster, and I thought I was really big stuff. "Yasu the drinker," they called me. In 1939 I was called up, and being rather wild to start with, I did some horrible things in China. I raped Chinese women. I knew if it got out that I'd raped them, I'd be punished. So I killed them. In 1942 I became a squad leader. I had a guy under me who was utterly loyal to me. If I did something wrong, *he'd* feel the pain. Our position was bombed, and while we were pulling back to new positions, we went for more than twenty days without food. We turned into wild animals; but this guy, he would dig up tree roots and give them to me to eat. Everyone was frantic, searching for something for himself to eat; and I was completely shameless and ate whatever he gave me without a second thought. Before we made it to the next position, the enemy hit us again. This man of mine lay on top of me and protected me with his own body; it's thanks to him that I'm alive. But I lost my hearing and my tongue froze up: I still had my voice but I couldn't make any words. And all the flesh on my right palm was gone. I was repatriated, and I recovered, but my right hand was useless, so they discharged me. I cried. The guy who gave up his life for me was still in my thoughts, and I wanted to go back to the battlefield and fight. I hadn't kept a single thing to remember him by: that's the kind of guy I'd been. I couldn't even spare the energy to blame myself for it. I was a wretched specimen, just clinging to my own life. I'm trying to make amends for that now. I've given up drinking and women.

As he finished, he showed me his hand, its fingers curled up like a bear's claw. Then he turned his back to me and fell fast asleep. I was ashamed I'd felt even the slightest bit wary of him.

After that, I always went with Yasu-san on foraging expeditions. Not once did he ever bother me or do anything cruel; he always looked after me kindly.

It was around the time when controls on foraging in the countryside had become tight, and I was picked up by a policeman. He took me back to the police station and told me he was going to confiscate my potatoes.

"If you think you're going to take these away, just try it! I'll hang myself right here in front of you, that's what! You think I do this for the fun of it? If I lose these we'll starve to death! Give them back!" My nose began to run, and I wailed and cried.

"That's no way for a nice girl like you to behave—here now, blow your nose!" The policeman handed me a tissue and sent me on my way. "But don't let us catch you at this again. I'm only doing my job; if I see you I can't let you get away with it. Today we'll pretend I didn't see you."

STREET STALL

When I was a geisha and a kept woman, I did know how terrifying other people could be, but I didn't know just how painful it was to work hard. As I've said before, working at the sawmill near my aunt's place was my first shock. Up until then, despite all else, I'd assumed that as long as I had a rice bowl, there'd be food to put in my mouth. But then I discovered that food was something that could be had only if you worked until you dropped.

The strain of working too hard finally took its toll, and in March of the year after I'd begun foraging in the countryside, I took to my bed for a week. I don't remember clearly what happened after that. At any rate, foraging for food to sell was heavy physical work; it was obvious that my body couldn't take it any longer.

One day when I was walking through the grounds of Chiba Shrine, I ran into Matsumura-san, a Korean I knew slightly, so I asked him if there wasn't some way I could make a bit of money. I felt like I was grasping at straws, but I got him to let me sell soap. In the grounds of the shrine was a lively outdoor black market, and most of the stall operators were Koreans.[2] I fell in with them.

"Right this way! Right this way! Top-class luxury soap for sale! Gentle to your hands! Look how rich and foamy it is!" I'd cry out, stopping people in their tracks and showing them how it foamed up. At first I found it hard to get my voice out. And although I claimed it wouldn't hurt your skin, in fact it did, so badly that it peeled off in sheets. It was terrible stuff that turned to mush in the space of three days. I bought it for 15 yen and sold it for 20.

The market was right on the border between heaven and hell. If you failed to grab a spot right in the center but were a little off to the side, you'd find yourself square in the middle of hell. It fairly teemed with terrifying goings-on such as you'd never see on the right side of the world.

"Hey girl! Got any smokes?" With an opening line something like this, one or other of a group of wannabe gangsters would come over and try to strike up conversation. My heart starts to pound, but if you let your fear show, it'll do you no good in the long run. I answer him with all the courage I can muster.

"I might have a few. But who are you with?"

"Don't give me that stuff! You're new here, aren't you girl?"

"Me? I'm not with anyone. I don't swing the kind of weight you guys do, either. Matsumura said I could set up here, that's all."

"Oh, I get it. You're his little piece of ass, eh?" one of them says, cocking his little finger at me knowingly.

"What's it to you, dearie? Here, want one?" I offer him a cigarette and take one for myself; but I can hardly keep my hand from trembling as I light it.

Almost every day there'd be an argument so violent it'd make the likes of me cringe with fear. But after a couple of months had passed, I became completely used to the life. I got the hang of making the pitch and was selling more and more soap.

Once I got to know the Koreans, I found them easy to get along with. When a group of them got together, they'd talk in booming voices, full of confidence; but on their own they were timid. Like a dog with its ears drooping and its tail between its legs, they'd shrink back as if to say, I surrender. I came to feel as if I were one of them. When they'd lose a fight, I'd be the one who'd feel bitter.

"Give it another go!" I'd say, stamping my feet on the ground. "The bastards! If only I were strong enough!"

GANG MOLL

I felt completely at home in the role of gang moll. One day, one of the gangsters, a guy of about thirty-four or thirty-five whom everyone looked up to as "Boss Gan," came over and for no good reason began to pick a fight with me.

"You want me to dump all this stuff on the ground for you?" he said, thumping his fist on the stand where I had the soap laid out.

If gangsters were always hanging around in front of my stall, no customers would come near me. I knew I had to have a word with him about this. So I put on my best imitation of a brazen face and said:

"So you're Gan, the big boss around here, eh? Well Boss, how's it gonna look if word gets around that big boy's been picking on little girls like me? What say you meet me at eight tonight at Inohanayama?" Inohanayama was around behind the shrine.

"All right, then. How many of you coming?" he answered.

"What the hell are you on about? I'm not coming to pick a fight with you! I'm coming to put a proposition to you. One to one. I just wanna talk to you, one human being to another; that's why I'm asking you."

If we couldn't reach an agreement that evening, I was determined to play my last card. Being the mistress of a gangster boss might be all right. I certainly had no sense of feminine virtue. I'd never been taught any. And even if I had, in the world I'd been living in, it would've been worth about as much as an empty pack of cigarettes.

Inohanayama was a heavenly place, full of camellias in bloom. I threw myself on the ground at Gan's feet. "Boss, I beg you! I've got a little brother who means more to me than my own life. You don't know how I've suffered for not having any education. I want to give my brother enough schooling so he can at least write his own name. Once I've done that, I don't care what happens to me. Until then, I want to stick to the straight and narrow. If I don't keep at it now, my brother'll quit school. I beg you, please, stand by me! It's the truth." I pressed my forehead into the dust.

"You know what pisses me off—that you, a Japanese, are the mistress of a Korean, that's what."

"I'm not! It's Matsumura's old lady who looks after me, not him. If you think I'm lying, go ask her! Until my little brother can stand on his own two feet, I've renounced men."

"All right, then. I'm with you. But if you're lying and I find out you've got a guy on the side, you won't get off lightly."

We parted and I returned home. That evening, I hacked off at the roots the waist-length hair that'd been so dear to me for so many years, and I offered it up to who-knows-which god at a small shrine that still survived in the burned-out remains of the main shrine. "No men until my brother can stand on his own two feet," I vowed.

Unawares, my brother slept peacefully through all this, but the next morning he was wide-eyed with astonishment.

"Sis, what have you done? Even your hair? It meant so much to you!"

"It's going to get hot; it'll just get in the way," I said nonchalantly and went off to the hairdresser to have it trimmed.

There's nothing you can't do if you throw yourself into it with all your heart. I managed to gain the support of those guys we call gangsters. Even they, once you get to know them, are good people. They're quick to anger, but if you treat them decently, more than likely they'll put their own head in the noose for you. I decided to throw a big party outside in the grounds of the shrine, and I invited all the gangsters and treated them to grilled dried cuttlefish and a big bottle of cheap liquor. Once my liquor was gone, they got together and brought out another big bottle; they laughed and sang and seemed to enjoy themselves. I played the gang moll and sat with my legs crossed, pretending I could drink as much as the best of them, but that liquor didn't agree with me at all.

I never let any of the guys I was friendly with come near the house; my brother was sensitive and I wanted to spare him any hurt. Yasu-san was the only one who was a good friend to my brother. He'd set a good example for him, I felt, and he'd be careful not to teach him anything bad.

One morning, about a year or so after I'd fallen in with this group, I went to work as usual, only to find everyone in an uproar because Gan had been stabbed. I found out which hospital he was in and hurried there. Gan was groaning in pain, and his girlfriend Masako was sitting, downcast, by his bed. The story was that the night before, three guys were passing on the street when suddenly they stabbed him and ran away. Luckily they'd got him in the appendix, so his life wasn't in danger, but Masako said she was worried because his intestines had been cut, too. Gan opened his eyes briefly and saw me, then began groaning in pain again.

"I don't get it. The great Gan down and out just because of a little cut? You ought to be ashamed of yourself! I've been hurt much worse, but I didn't cry or moan. Look at this!" I said, pushing my leg with its scar right up in front of his eyes.

Masako was the one who was shocked. "How on earth did you get that?"

"This? Well, when I was small, there was this demon, you see, and this demon threw me down a flight of stairs. See, here's proof. There really are demons in this world, and they left this here to prove it." I'd grown so bold I could say things like that with a straight face; I had to chuckle at how pleased I was with my own daring. "Pull yourself together! You're not gonna die!" I said to him as I left the hospital.

LITTLE FOUNDLING

Matsumura-san's old lady was worried about me. "You better not get too involved with these people, you know. What'll you do if you can't get away from them?"

I smiled and told her not to worry. "I'll be all right. I know what I'm up to. It's not as if I've drunk a pledge of allegiance to them or even agreed to be their gang moll. They're just looking after me, that's all."

In fact, as long you took things as they came without fretting too much about it, you could get them to see your point of view. There was more of the sweetheart in them than the swaggerer. It's true, though, that they were a bit short of intelligence. But the really tough types wouldn't be hanging around the grounds of some shrine; they'd be doing something a bit more profitable. These guys would blow in a single night the tiny bit of cash they'd earned in prison; then, flat broke, they'd break into an empty house, steal something, try to pawn it, and get caught. Then they'd steal a locked bicycle, hoist it onto their shoulders, stagger away, and get caught again. They'd spend the night at an inn, and the next morning get caught walking out with the bedding on their backs: one more offense. With this careless crime and that, some of them had six or more convictions to their credit.

There was this orphan called Sute-chan, "Little Foundling," who worked for a Korean shoe peddler. The kid often said how much he hated the shoe man, so I arranged for him to be taken on by a sea-weed shop in Goi. The day that he left, I said to him, "You're not to come back here, OK? If something happens and you just can't take it, you tell me first." Wishing him good luck, I sent him off with a bundle of my little brother's old underwear and clothing.

Some six months later, word came that he'd been picked up by the police. They say that he and his friends had stolen something from the seaweed shop, sold it, and were carousing on the proceeds when they were caught.

I ran to the police, but they sent me away, saying that visiting hours were over. At eight the next morning I went again, and after being kept waiting for ages, was finally permitted to see him. The police station was a grim place; just a table and three chairs in a room, and a policeman keeping watch from the side as Sute and I sat facing each other. "Might we ask you to leave us alone?" I asked; but the policeman only made a sour face and shook his head. There was no way I could say what I wanted to say. I looked Sute-chan in the eye and said, "All right, tell me the truth. You won't lie to me, Sute-chan, will you? If you stole something, that's OK. I promise I won't be angry. Tell me why you did it. All I want is to hear what's on your mind."

Sute-chan began crying bitterly. "Me? I didn't steal nothing. The older boys told me they'd treat me to something nice to eat," he said hesitantly. "I just went along with them." His eyes told me this was the truth.

The policeman told me my ten minutes of visiting time was up. I glared back at him and continued talking. "Sute-chan, were you drinking?"

"Drinking? No way! I was just eating."

"That's what I thought. I believe you. Don't you worry."

Once I'd heard the full story from Sute-chan, I went to the room where the policemen gathered to sort things out. "Could you possibly tell me exactly what it was that Sute did?"

"Who the hell are you?"

"Sute's older sister."

"Sute doesn't have any relatives."

"What's that you say? I'm his older sister. You mean we can't be brother and sister unless we have the same parents and are listed in the same family register? There are people born of the same parents who get on worse than strangers! But if you care for each other as we do and think of yourselves as brother and sister, then you are brother and sister. I know this kid better than anyone else. You've got to investigate this fully!"

"What're you going on about? We brought him in from the place where he and his friends were carousing."

"Carousing? You mean Sute was drinking?"

"Drinking or not, he was with them. His friends have admitted the crime. You've no grounds for complaint."

Even this doesn't faze me. From my days as a geisha, I'm used to nonentities who put on airs of importance. We argue back and forth until finally one of them loses his temper. "Listen, you! You're guilty too, right? You seem awfully full of yourself. You wanna stay here for two or three days until you cool off?"

"If you think you're gonna put me away, just try it. I've come here to rescue someone, and not in ten or twenty years am I gonna be stopped. As soon as I get out, I'll go to a higher authority, and if they won't listen to me, I'll go tell the whole world how great the Japanese police are! Acting like you're pulling on the legs of a hanged man—you'll regret it. Treat Sute as a criminal, just try it! I'll bring the wrath of heaven down on you, instantly! Some of you here must have kids of your own. Have you ever thought how you'd feel if this happened to one of them? Beasts! I thought the police would understand, but I was wrong." I totally lose my temper and can't stop my rage from boiling over.

One of them says soothingly, "Now, now, there's no point in getting so excited. We'll investigate things to your satisfaction, so you go on home now." There were some whose job it was to get angry and some who were there to appease you—I was impressed with how cleverly the police managed things.

Two days later I was summoned by the police. "We'll release Sute. In return, he's your responsibility. If Sute does anything wrong, you'll be charged with the same crime," they threatened. I nodded obediently. You be careful what you say, they told me; and to whatever else they said, I bowed and scraped, gushed thanks and empty compliments, until finally I scurried out with my tail between my legs.

That night I had Sute stay over at our place, and the next morning I met with the owner of the seaweed shop and managed to persuade him that Sute wasn't guilty of anything. The whole business had wasted two days of my time, but I was as happy as if I'd made a million yen. For dinner that night my little brother made do with the seaweed they'd given me, and then after he'd got into bed, he said thoughtfully, "Compared with Sute-chan, I'm lucky."

"Why's that?"

"Because I've got you, Sis. When I finish school, I'm gonna work real hard and pay you back. Poor Sute-chan, he's all alone in the world."

"No one's all alone, you know. Aren't we all surrounded by lots of good people?" I spoke as if I didn't know what he really meant, but I couldn't help myself and was weeping uncontrollably.

Seven funerary laths

I spent two and a half years selling soap at Chiba Shrine, becoming totally involved in the lives of Matsumura-san and the other Koreans, sharing their joy and anger, sadness and pleasure. I became used to their flamboyant domestic disputes, their custom of wailing at the top of their voices when someone died; and I learned how to make beaten barley cakes and distill liquor.

My brother finished school without incident. Around that time the high-quality soap used by the Occupation Forces began to appear on the market, with the result that the inferior stuff, which turns to mush after only three days, became harder to sell in town. I took my brother with me and went to sell it out in the country.

On the first day, we took a chance and hopped the first bus that turned up at Chiba Keisei station. At the end of the line we got off and separated, each of us setting out in a different direction to sell our soap. The last bus back was at ten past six, so we decided we'd meet again at half-past five at the place where we'd parted.

"Need any soap today?" I'd say as I stepped through the gate.

"Nope!" I was refused at every house, with looks as if they were chasing away a thieving cat. By the time I'd been turned away from the third house, my face should have grown skin as thick as a cast-iron griddle; but when I came to the next house, I began to falter. It was one in the afternoon, and I hadn't sold a single bar. The June sun beat down relentlessly, and I began to feel tired and fed up. My poor brother, out hawking for the first time! How wretched and humiliated he must feel. He may even have gone back to the pine grove where we're to meet, I thought; so when one house bought two bars, I took that as my cue to go back and have a look. He wasn't there. I ate my lunch and then lay down flat on my back, arms outstretched, looking up at the sky through the pine needles, wondering what on earth had become of him. All I could hear was the sighing of the wind in the branches. What a tranquil place this is, I thought; how pleasant it would be to go to sleep forever in a place like this; and in the midst of this reverie, I fell sound asleep. When suddenly I woke, it was already four o'clock.

I trudged off toward the bus stop. He wasn't there either. It was after five o'clock when he came back, grinning from ear to ear and dripping with sweat, carrying a load on his back that towered above his head.

"Hey sis! How about a sweet potato? I thought, sweet potatoes, oh no! They're so heavy! But I made the trade anyhow."

"That's all sweet potatoes?"

"Of course not. There's rice and beans and all sorts of stuff."

After we got on the bus, he rummaged around for a bit and then said, "Want one?" holding out a steamed sweet potato wrapped in newspaper. It was completely squashed and shapeless, but as I ate it I was deeply touched by the realization that my brother was now a grown-up. That night, even after we'd eaten, he was still lining up the things he'd managed to get hold of all by himself.

"Sis, if we take these to Matsumura-san's tomorrow, they're sure to buy them. In my experience, you know, rich people in big houses are no good. It's the small houses that'll buy. Business is perseverance, isn't it?" he said, crowing with delight. "It's not luck, that's for sure." Seeing my brother in such a mood, I too felt spurred to new efforts.

It was about this time that Elder Sister Karuta suddenly announced that she was going back to Shinshū. Her *danna* had been paralyzed by a stroke, and his wife was the jealous type, endlessly fretting and fuming. It was just one irksome problem after another, and she couldn't put up with it any longer. If he were to die, everything she had invested in him would be lost. It'd be wiser, she said, to take whatever money she could lay her hands on now, even though it wasn't much, go back to the town where she was born, and do something there.

"Why don't you two come along? If you go back home, surely there'll be some way of making a living," she said. But to me, Shinshū meant nothing but bitter memories. Even the recollection of him, the man I'd loved as if my very life depended on it, now aroused no more than an occasional prick of pain deep within my breast. All I hoped for was that my little brother and I could save up enough money to buy a stall in the market, no matter how small, where we could start a business of some sort.

We'd got used to beaten barley cakes and cheap liquor, to taking whatever we could get our hands on into the countryside and trading it for anything we could bring back and sell. In those days, I'd become a perfect demon for money: anything I thought would make money, I'd do. People seemed to find me rather useful; if I was asked to get them some rice by a certain day, or some barley, I'd get it. In this way, we survived.

Then I heard that if you collected the heads of forty-nine funerary laths, each one from the middle lath of a set of seven, your wish would be granted.[3] My brother and I went out collecting them in the middle of the night. It's no easy task to find the middle lath of a set of seven, but we were determined to have a stall in the market, and finally we collected them. I still have the ashes from when we burned them.

It had been five years since I'd severed my ties with rouge and face powder, but perhaps there was still a trace of femininity about me. For occasionally someone would make eyes at me, squeeze my hand, and say, "Look love, someone as young as you shouldn't have to work so hard. There are easier ways, you know, any number of 'em."

When that happened, I'd fend them off politely. "I'm very grateful for your kindness, but please don't touch my hand. My body is rotting and your hand will rot, too." But if they persisted, I could put some fight into it. "Don't mess with me, you bastard. Keep your filthy hands off me or I'll throttle you."

And so I managed to save up a bit of money, little though it was, and it looked as if our hopes were just on the point of materializing. Then, in the summer of 1952, my brother suddenly said that his stomach hurt and took to his bed. At first I was so engrossed in making money that I didn't pay much attention; but he seemed to have a fever, too, so I had the doctor come round and examine him. It was intestinal tuberculosis, he said, and if he wasn't admitted to hospital soon, he could die. I had him admitted to the Chiba Medical School Hospital just as quickly as I could manage it, and for a while I stayed with him there; but in no time at all our savings had evaporated, and I had to leave my brother alone in the hospital and go to work.

Chapter 8 🙢 The Depths of Despair

MY LITTLE BROTHER'S SUICIDE

Looking back on it, the reason I'd been able to live so steadfast and pure a life these past few years, despite my poverty, was precisely because I had my brother's support. Now that he had fallen ill, my old energy evaporated. Small wonder that I spent all my time in a daze, never leaving the hospital, until I hadn't a single sen left.

But when I did come to my senses, I realized that having to earn the price of penicillin at 600 yen per shot wouldn't be easy for me. Even working as much as I possibly could, I'd be hard put to make enough for one shot in three days. Finally, at my wit's end and telling myself it was the quickest way to make money, I went to work in a place called Hasuike, the local "flower-and-willow" district. By that time, geisha too were no longer what they had been before the war; they had become no more than mere prostitutes. Nights I worked and the days I spent with my brother in the hospital.

"Money? Matsumura-san will lend me as much as I need, so . . ." That was the story I told my brother. But he was no longer a child, and—did he know everything? On the night of the twelfth of October, after I had left for work, he threw himself off the roof of the hospital.

> Sister, I don't want to burden you any more than I have already. My life can't be saved in any case. Father died of this disease, too. I remember how pitifully Mother struggled then, trying to cure him. Sister, please, let yourself have a happier life.[1]

This was the note he left behind.

I rushed there in a frenzy, and in that instant in the operating room, when I was shown my brother's mangled body, I felt as if all the blood in my own body had begun to flow backward. My head was empty; the only thing I could feel was something tiny in there going round and round and round. I wanted to cry but no tears would come, and in the end I began to laugh hysterically.

Everyone says that I went mad. If I'd really gone mad, I might have been happy, but I was quite sane. Day after day I would sit in my room staring into space, drinking nothing, eating nothing, just crying and muttering to myself. "I don't care if you rip off my arms and legs and make a Daruma doll of me. Just give me back my brother!"[2] I'd shriek, pleading with no one in particular. That's what they told me, but I don't really remember. I knew that I had to think, that I had to concentrate on something; but a hollow had formed in my head, and I was incapable of thinking about anything. I couldn't but begrudge my brother the courage it took to jump from such a high place.

"Masaru! Did you really think I could be happy without you?" Didn't the child understand how I felt?

Mrs. Matsumura, Yasu-san, Gan, all of them worried about me and brought over food. And although I knew it wouldn't change anything, I just couldn't keep myself from yelling at them, "So you think if I eat this my brother'll come back, do you?"

Behind the medical school was a big tree of some sort that was forked at about the height of my chest; one fork had been cut off. Every night when I was looking after my brother, I would put my hand on that cut and pray that it would make me happy like other people. I did this because someone once told me that big trees bring happiness to people. Now I even went to vent my spleen against this tree. "I begged you for the happiness I craved," I told it. "If you really have divine powers, why didn't you stop my brother from killing himself? I hate you!"

For about a month I wandered like a sleepwalker, doing nothing, powerless to do anything. The Matsumuras forced me to come back to their house. "Now that you're all alone," they said kindly, "there's even more reason that you should become our child." If I went out, they had one of their children follow me, and if I shut myself up at my own place, they would keep watch on me there, all day long if necessary. They weren't going to let me do anything foolish, they said, and their efforts on my behalf, when I wasn't even the same nationality as them, moved me to tears. Once, when I hadn't eaten anything for two days, Mrs. Matsumura started crying.

"If you won't eat, then I won't eat either. If you don't care whether I die, then go ahead, see if I care!" Now threatening, now comforting me, she got me to eat.

For some time I felt as if I were living in a world without sound and without light. I want to die, I thought; how wonderful it would be if I could die. But these were only empty thoughts; I hadn't the courage to do anything about it.

RETURN TO SUWA

At any rate, I wanted to bury my brother next to Father, so I left Chiba. Even now in my mind's eye, I can see Mrs. Matsumura seeing me off at Shinjuku Station in her white Korean dress, saying over and over again, "Promise you'll come back! Promise you'll be my child!" Up to the very last moment before I left, everyone did their best not to upset me, handling me as gently as if they were treating an abscess.

When I got back to Shiojiri, I kept a single 1,000-yen note for myself and gave the rest to my aunt, telling her that I'd be staying for a while.

The next day I went to Father's grave, and with my hands and a stick, I worked a long time digging a hole in which I buried my brother's bones. Then I replaced the earth, singing lullabies all the while, and stayed there until it got dark. After that I went to the grave every day and sang lullabies. I felt that it was the least I could do by way of an offering for the repose of his soul, for a brother who had never heard a lullaby from his own mother.

Everyone in the village seemed to think I had gone stark raving mad. Apparently they told my aunt that it terrified them to hear lullabies when they passed along the road below the graveyard. Even when the wind was raging or the snow was falling, I would still go out to the graveyard. In doing that, I felt, I was at least registering my protest against all of them. "Which of you ever did anything for that poor sweet boy?" I thought to myself.

Before long, it was New Year's 1953. There had been a great storm, and the mound of earth over my brother's grave was buried under snow. I was not in good health, and it was bitterly cold. I had to give up my daily visits to the grave, and so I decided to go to Suwa.

I had no idea what I would do once I got to Suwa, but I suppose I did want to see the lake. For the first time in ages I decided I'd comb my hair, but when I looked in the mirror it made my blood run cold. My face was wan, my eyes haggard—no doubt about it, I thought, this is the visage of a madwoman.

In Suwa, the town was bustling with New Year's activity. The willows on the bank, the Inari Shrine, my "secret place," everything was just as it had been before. Mother and Father from the Takenoya had, I heard, moved to Kobe. I went to see the mistress of the Ichiriki.

"What on earth happened to you? Where have you been? You look like a ghost—well, do come in!" She welcomed me much more warmly than I'd expected, firing questions at me as fast as she could get the words out.

"That Motoyama-san you were rumored to be seeing, he's come back, you know, and he's a city councillor now." She told me this as cheerfully as if it were her own news.

So he's back. But it was too distant a memory to be pleased about. What with one painful struggle after another to contend with, I hadn't had a moment even to think about him.

That evening I collapsed with a high fever and had to sleep at the Ichiriki. I had caught a cold at my aunt's place and shouldn't have pushed myself to do so much.

REUNION

I'd been beset by bad dreams, one nightmare after another; but when I opened my eyes, who should I see but Motoyama-san sitting by my bed. At first I thought I must still be dreaming; but when he gently shook my shoulder, I realized that it really was him. I couldn't imagine how desperately he had searched for me, he told me bitterly. Four years ago he'd given up and got married, and he had a child, he confessed. For my part, I'd never entertained any hope of marrying him; so I was overjoyed just to see him again.

He said it hadn't been until much later that he'd heard from the mistress of the Ichiriki that I'd gone to Chiba; and when I noticed his expression suddenly turn dark, I sensed that he'd also heard about my dancing naked. But he didn't broach the subject, and I was painfully conscious of how much he cared for me.

From then on he looked after me, making sure I lacked for nothing, and before three days had passed, he'd found me a place to live and taken me there. Whenever he came by, he'd bring one thing and another that he'd bought for me; he even bought me a radio, thinking I must be lonely living there all by myself.

It wasn't long before the cherry trees were in bloom and I had completely recovered. As inconspicuously as possible, we went together to see the blossoms at night. I hadn't realized that cherry blossoms could be this beautiful. Until then, I'd walked around with my eyes fixed on the ground; I had no room in my life to enjoy anything like cherry blossoms. Beautiful! Beautiful! I sighed deeply and drank them in as if I were seeing cherry blossoms for the first time.

The next day I went out alone and, taking care to let no one see me, I climbed up one of the cherry trees. The blossoms were in full bloom. Honeybees buzzed busily about. Spiders were repairing damage to their webs. They all were alive. I was alive and so glad to be that I wanted to give thanks, to something.

On nights when the moon shone beautifully, we sometimes arranged to meet by the lake, just like old times. When human beings are at the height of happiness or in the depths of despair—then, I thought at the time, the moon and stars appear strangely beautiful. Happiness was mine again. Even just a glimpse of his face was enough to make me say, "I'm happy."

Often he would take me in his arms and say tearfully, "You're happy just with this? I feel I've done you wrong. No matter how I feel, though, it's too late to do anything about it. How I regret getting married so hastily!"

But I didn't think of myself as someone you could call a mistress. And my landlady said she didn't think of me as a mistress; that pleased me. "No married couple can compare with you. You're a joy to behold! When two young people love each other, they make everyone who sees them feel good."

There were no ropes or chains to bind me now. I was free, and I could love him just as I wished. I'd never dreamed that such a day would come my way.

HAPPY DAYS

Every month on the twelfth I went to pray at my brother's grave. When Motoyama-san would come with me, on the way home we would enjoy ourselves picking bracken shoots at Shiojiri Pass or, in the autumn, gathering mushrooms.

Once it happened that I lost sight of him in the mountains, and no matter how I called him, there was no answer. It reminded me of those times when I'd stood alone by Lake Suwa, and I broke down and cried. At that point he appeared, smiling, and said, "I hid so I could watch you." I clung to him and blubbered like a child. "What a big baby you are! Well, come on then," he said, and hoisted me on his back and carried me through the mountains.

At New Year's, he wanted to see me with my hair up, Japanese style, so for the first time in ages I had it done up. I made such a fuss about how heavy it was that he began to laugh. Also at his suggestion, I began to teach myself, whenever I was alone, how to write—a-i-u-e-o, beginning right from the start. And then I learned how to record the things I'd thought and felt, writing them down, day by day, in a notebook. When I think back, even from this distance, I'm struck by what happy days they were, as if bathed in bright sunlight. Reading now what I wrote then, there's not a single sad moment:

__ Month __ Day

He has business in Matsumoto and I go with him. I play with the pigeons around the lanterns of a shrine while waiting for him to finish his business. He buys a cotton kimono for me for 1,050 yen, we see a movie, have dinner at Ippei, and come back.

__ Month __ Day

Today we went to my brother's grave and then enjoyed ourselves at Shiojiri Pass. We had a singing contest, but he's tone-deaf, and listening to him I had to burst out laughing. It was rude of me and I regret it. I sang in such a loud voice that it echoed through the mountains, and I danced Spring Rain for him.

___ Month ___ Day

Today I spent the whole day watching sparrows make a nest. In the evening, he didn't come over, so I had dinner at my landlady's place. Afterward, I played snap with her and her husband. She loves playing snap, and whenever the three of us happen to be together, she'll get out the deck of cards and say let's play.

___ Month ___ Day

Today someone I hadn't seen for ages came over. Elder Sister Temari paid me a visit. We talked and talked about old times, and Temari stayed the night.

She'd been married. But she'd run out on him. Marriage? she says; marriage just means having your arms and legs shackled and your freedom taken away, it's no fun at all. If you're together all day every day, you're forced to see his ugly side, too, like it or not. But living like this, as you do, you see only his good side, and you don't get sick of him. Married life? It's good for at most six months. Once a year has passed, you're just disillusioned.

It's been ages, she says; let's go for a walk around Suwa. So we go into town, and strolling aimlessly about, we come to the base of the tree that we used to climb to our secret place, and she insists that we climb it. Come off it, we're not children any more, I protest; but she just won't listen. There was nothing for it, so I took off the cord under my obi and hooked it to a lower branch, and with that to help us, and a lot of hard work, we barely managed to boost each other up the tree. Then—what possessed her, I can't imagine—she starts peeing, whoosh, whoosh. Ah, that feels great, she says, just as cool as can be; let's go home now.

Oh, Elder Sister, there's no one quite like you. I was still laughing when we got home. As we said good-bye she urged me, over and over, not to let this happiness get away from me. You're going to hold on to it, hold tight! she said as she left.

FAREWELL BANQUET

I tended to forget that Motoyama-san had a wife and child. Yet happy though we'd been, I began to sense as autumn approached that he was depressed about something.

"Is something wrong?" I'd ask.

"Nothing worth worrying about. But what about you? Are you happy? How did you pass the time today?" He would always respond by trying to comfort me instead. I couldn't get anything out of him. But I knew there must be something the matter, and I passed the days in a state of nervous apprehension.

I even imagined he might be sad just because it was autumn. But finally the day came when this happy dream was mercilessly demolished. His wife came to see me. When I saw her standing there before my very eyes, I got quite a shock, as you might imagine, and my knees were trembling. But I kept a firm grip on myself and stood up to her. "What are you doing here?"

She looked down and tears welled in her eyes. "I've come prepared to be made a fool of. I've suffered, too, but now my husband's suffering so badly that I've come to beg you. The fact is that his term of office on the city council is over and elections are drawing near. I'm embarrassed to admit it, but we don't have much money, and when he approached the people who supported him in the past, they gave him a terrible tongue-lashing and told him they couldn't support a man who'd lost his head over a woman. Couldn't you break off with him, even just for a little while? If it's you who makes him happy, then as soon as this thing's over I'll take the child and go away. But just for now, so my husband can keep his job, I beg you."

There wasn't a hint of resentment in anything she said. She turned and left, and as I watched that forlorn figure disappear, I was deeply ashamed that I'd been so aggressive. But could I have wounded him that deeply? I love him, too. So why should I give a damn? Go to hell! But what becomes of the child then? To steal the father of an innocent child is just too horrid. For if that means creating another person who'd suffer the same anguish as I did . . .

After countless sleepless nights, tortured by my own selfish attachments, and feeling as if the very thought could make me bleed, I reached a decision. To leave him was, ultimately, the fate decreed for me; precisely because I loved him, I had to leave him.

On the night that I'd determined would be our last before I left him, I prepared a simple farewell banquet. He did his utmost not to let his anguish show. I did my utmost not to let him know of my decision. Because we loved each other, we fought back our tears as we quietly dined; it was a gloomy banquet. That night I clung to him, determined that if a woman's life could be burned out in a single night, then tonight I'd burn mine out. Tonight was the last time I'd pillow my head on his arm, his chest. Why must I be the only one to lose the man I'd loved like this; to bear this pain? Determined to brand the vision of his face on my heart, I spent the night staring at his slumbering face, never sleeping a wink.

LOVE'S ANGUISH

I left a letter for him with my landlady, called for a car, and loaded all my luggage into it, then left for Toyoshina. It was toward the end of 1954. In Toyoshina, Elder Sister Karuta had opened a restaurant, and at first I stayed with her.[3]

After I arrived I still couldn't break the bonds of my insane attachment to him; I hardly knew what to do with myself. Not a day passed that I didn't reek of saké. When I got drunk I yearned for him; when I sobered up I yearned for him all the more. I was writhing and squirming like a snake left for dead but still alive. I'd see a man who looked like *him* and spend the night with him; that's how stupid I'd become. Of course those men who looked so much like him weren't him, they just looked like him. And afterward I'd feel like I'd been chewing on ashes; no matter how I'd try to spit it out, the bad taste still remained.

No doubt a virtuous woman, firm in her chastity, could have lived by embracing just a vision of him; but I was a fool. Knowing full well that I'd be left in pain, I persisted in my stupidity. In aimless pursuit of a phantasm, I'd spend the night with this one and that, then in the morning find my foulness unbearable. The tears would stream down my face, reflected in the mirror, and I'd laugh derisively. Even surrounded by drunken customers, clapping in time to the music, I'd feel as lonely as if I were wandering in a wasteland. With all my heart I wished I could escape from this pain and suffering just as quickly as I could; if only there were an Aladdin's Lamp and it could exchange human hearts for new ones, how I wished I could exchange mine. Yet for all my vain hopes, I was incapable of doing anything for myself. Sodden with saké, abandoning myself to a life of despair, both my heart and my body went to ruin.

My face had become bloated, and then my arms and legs swelled up. Often I would feel a pain just below my breast, as if a drill were driving into me. I'd get the doctor to give me a shot of morphine, which would relieve the pain for a time, yet despite all this I was still drinking constantly. The doctor told me I was doing dreadful damage to my liver, that this stupidity would cost me my life. I was delighted. For one as deeply sinful as I was, it would be a blessing to die of disease.

By now my face had turned yellow with jaundice. The doctor was furious with me. "If you don't quit drinking, you really will die. As a doctor, there's nothing more I can do for you. A patient who knows full well she's killing herself is a patient I can do without. They'll only say I've killed you, so I wash my hands of you."

"If that's how you feel, that's just fine with me!" I spat back at him. "The world's littered with doctors anyway." I'd drink and throw myself into the pond in the middle of the night, climb trees and scream; I was out of control.

Finally Karuta lost her temper. "For you that may be just fine, to be so pigheaded that you die, but what about me? They'll say I killed you because I didn't get you to a doctor. If you're so determined to die, then go and die somewhere else! I haven't said anything so far because I know how you're hurting, but a nitwit like you'd be better off dead!"

I knew this wasn't what she really felt. It was her way of being kind, of getting me to see a doctor and making me quit drinking. But I was in no condition to accept her kindness for what it was. "All right then, I'm leaving! That's fine with you, I presume?" I grabbed all the money I had and stalked out.

HAPPINESS AND UNHAPPINESS

I jumped onto the bus for Matsumoto, determined that this time I really would die. This time I'll freeze to death, I decided; they say it's an easy death; but first I headed for my brother's grave. When I arrived in Matsumoto, I found it would be an hour's wait for the train to Shiojiri and half an hour for the bus. There was nothing else I could so, so I sat down in the waiting room; but the moment I did, I felt that stabbing pain below my breast again. I had a doctor in the neighborhood give me an injection; but for two or three hours after an injection, I would fall sound asleep, no matter how hard I tried to stay awake. So straightaway I got a taxi and had the driver take me to Asama, the hot springs where I'd stayed a couple of times with *him*.

At Asama I collapsed and slept for two days; then on the afternoon of the third day, as snowflakes fluttered down, I went outside. I was walking aimlessly toward the bus stop when someone called out to me. "Elder Sister Crane? Is that you?" I looked searchingly at the woman. She was wearing an apron so grimy it was impossible to tell if it had ever been white. Her hair was gray with dust. Her face was covered with freckles, and her yellowed teeth stuck out as she stood there, grinning at me. The child on her back looked as if it had only just been born. "I'm sorry, but what was your name?"

"You're Elder Sister Crane, aren't you? I'm Fusako." It was Little Fusa who'd been the nursemaid at the hairdresser's. I was quite at a loss for words. "Do come on over," she demanded. "It's so good to see you." I was so lonely I went along with her.

I was shocked at what I found. Could such a place as this be called a home? She said it was her husband's elder brother's house. At the side of the house they'd built a lean-to using scraps of lumber for the roof and straw matting for the walls. The place where we entered was the kitchen and beyond it was a six-mat room, in a corner of which some threadbare quilts were piled up; next to them were two tea chests, and on top of one of them was a wicker trunk with a hole in it. This seemed to be all they possessed.

"Sorry there's no proper cushion," Little Fusa said as she sat me down. "There's nothing I can offer you, but that's all right, isn't it? Do have some tea before you go, though." She began busying herself in the kitchen. Three little boys, so close in age that I couldn't tell who was the eldest and who the youngest, gathered round, staring vacantly at me. I'd just noticed the scent of cooking when she produced a plate piled high with slices of potato simmered in *miso*. I was deeply impressed at the speed with which she'd put together something for me with what little she had on hand.

"What does your husband do?" I knew that probably was the wrong thing to say, but I couldn't help asking.

"He's a day laborer. We've got a lot of kids, so he works hard. Today he's gone to chop firewood, and at 7 yen a bundle he's got to chop fifty bundles at least, he said, and won't be back; or not until after dark, I s'pose. I'll go out to work once the kids are old enough to play by themselves, and then things'll be a bit easier, I s'pose. But sometimes I get work washing cotton kimono at inns. I like to earn a little something toward our keep."

"Sure. You look happy, you know."

"Happy? Come off it! Not without a sen to our names we're not! But we'll manage somehow 'til the kids have grown up. That's the only thing we've got to look forward to."

One of the children began to pester her. "Ma, I want a rice ball with *miso* on it!" Me too! Me too! the other two joined in. "All right then." Little Fusa got up. "The kids love *miso* rice balls; so as long as we've got *miso* and rice, we don't need anything else," she laughed. But in my heart I knew that it wasn't that the children loved *miso*; even they realized there wasn't anything else to eat.

"You don't have to go yet, do you? Pa'll be glad to see you when he gets back. Why don't you stay a bit longer?" But I brushed off her attempts to keep me there and set off as if in flight. It had disoriented me to see something so unexpected in a place where I least expected it; yet at the same time I began to think about the forms that human happiness, and unhappiness, might take, and where they might be found. Had I merely caught sight of her as I passed by, traipsing along in her worn-down wooden sandals, with the four children in tow, probably I'd only have scowled and thought, "How wretched." Yet here was a woman made rich at heart by the hopes and peace of mind she could look forward to when her children grew up. As I left, I'd wrapped up 2,000 yen and pressed it into her hand, saying, "Buy something for the kids." She'd be unwrapping it about now, probably in a transport of delight and surprise to see how much she'd received.[4] In my mind's eye, I could see her happiness.

But what about me? A small diamond sparkled on my finger. And I had a gold watch. On my feet, a pair of leather sandals. In my purse, I had 4,000 or 5,000 yen left. But despite this, my soul was starving, thirsting, crazed with agony as it roamed about looking for a place to die.

Wandering between life and death

When I boarded the bus from Shiojiri, a heavy snow began to fall, and I gave up all hope that I might catch a glimpse of Lake Suwa from Shiojiri Pass. I got off the bus en route, at the entrance to Tagawaura Mineral Springs. Here the mountains were densely massed even for Shinshū, a place where not a soul was to be seen in winter.

As I headed into the hills, determined to die if I could, I began to wander with no particular destination in mind. When I plunged into the forest, I was buried above my knees in snow. I took off my sandals and walked on, barefoot. The chill soon passed, and before long I lost all feeling in my hands and feet. I'd heard people say that when you walk about like this you begin to feel sleepy; but I only got soaked and started to shiver; I didn't feel the least bit sleepy. Shit, am I never going to feel sleepy? Now I was crying and growing ever more exasperated.

I don't know how long it took, but my eyes had gone bleary and I was all but unconscious. And then, in a mountain hut about four kilometers from the bus stop, I was rescued by an old man of nearly eighty. He'd lit a fire and warmed me up all over; and after he listened to everything I had to say, he said, "When people think only of themselves, that's when they're most unhappy. Why don't you try doing something for someone else; just once in your life, that's enough. At any rate, give it one more year. And during that year, just once, do something to make someone else happy. If you still want to die, then come back here. If you do that, I'll help you die painlessly."

The old man told me that many years ago he'd been a member of the Communist Party and had been thrown into jail in Hokkaido.

But he'd broken out, and while he was on the run he'd despaired of life and sought death. He put me up for the night, and the next day when I went outside, there was this pair of ducks that he kept. I guess they thought a stranger like me looked suspicious, and they started quacking something ferocious. He said he kept them instead of a guard dog. I was amazed to hear that ducks could be trained to do the work of a dog.

Chapter 9   The Road Back to Life

INNOCENT SMILE

When I returned to Toyoshina, I pondered the old man's advice and tried my best to live up to it. But what could *I* possibly do—I who hadn't even been able to help myself? At this thought, another wave of misery would overwhelm me, which I was powerless to do anything about.

On one such day, on my way back from the doctor, I noticed a group of children looking at their storybooks and enjoying themselves immensely. "Lucky kids!" I thought to myself, and having nothing better to do, I stopped to have a look. One child, sitting apart from the others, caught my attention.

"What's the matter?" I asked.

"I ain't gotta book, so they won't play with me," he said and then ran away.

The scene had quite slipped my mind; but when I got into bed at night, just before I fell asleep, I would always say "Goodnight, Masaru," to the vision of my little brother. And as I whispered automatically "Goodnight, Masaru," I suddenly recalled the child who didn't have any books. Surely my brother, too, had had just such experiences, poor thing; and it occurred to me then to buy a book for the child.

The next day I bought a book and set out for the place I'd been the day before, but no one was there. I'd never cared for movies and books myself and never looked at either of my own accord, but even I was captivated by this comic book. Since I'd gone to the trouble to buy the thing I didn't want it to go to waste, so the following day I went again, but there was no one there. It was four or five days later that I encountered a child of about eight, snot running from his nose down over his lips, and he was crying. Dear oh dear! I said as I wiped his nose; then I handed him the book. "Here, this is for you." He stopped crying and retreated a few steps. "It's an interesting book, you know," I said; and when I insisted he take it, he opened his eyes wide and smiled at last. He really looked pleased. I felt jubilant as I walked home.

When I was a nursemaid in the home of the landowners, a nun who happened to pass once gave me something square and white. Timidly I licked it and discovered that it was sweet and delicious. I realize now that it must have been a sugar cube; but still, more than twenty years later, I remember clearly the joy I felt then. It's not just children; everyone seems to be deeply touched by unexpected joy brought to them by others and is unable to forget it.

That child will be grown up by now, and if he hasn't forgotten me, whenever he sees a crying child he'll want to say a kind word and wipe the kid's nose. And when that kid grows up, he'll do the same. To do something kind for another is never a bad feeling; it fosters a spirit of caring for other people. And who knows, after a few hundred years have passed, human beings may even learn to cooperate with one another. What a lovely place to live this world would be if only people would feel affection for everyone else, and all the ugliness of the human heart were to vanish—our envy of those better off than ourselves and our scorn for those worse off. Yes, that was it: I'd try to teach children that if they felt glad when someone gave them even a single piece of candy, then they in turn should give to others. Once I'd hit on this idea, I got started. I bought three comic books, and if I'd see some children I'd call them over—"Come here, come here, I'll show you a book!"—and share some sweets with them and get them in a good mood.

But the children soon tired of the same three books. There was nothing for me to do but to buy some more. With one thing and another, it was costing me 100 yen a day. My shot of gulonic acid cost 200 yen.[1] As a waitress in the restaurant, I earned 2,000 yen a week. No matter how good a moneymaker I might be, I couldn't make ends meet. At that point it occurred to me to make up my own children's stories and tell them instead. All the stories I'd heard and knew, the children knew much better. "No, Auntie, that's not how it goes. It's like this!" They ended up correcting me. And they told me that every children's story you could think of was already in the school library; so I decided to surprise them by making up something myself that they might enjoy. Here's one of my bumbling productions:

Piiko the Fledgling Hawk

Piiko the fledgling hawk didn't have a real father and mother. And so she was raised by human beings. Piiko's legs were chained together, and she spent all her time alone. "How I'd love to play with other birds!" she thought; but whenever other birds saw her, they flew away. Her only friends were the boy Masao and the kitten Miiko. But Masao went off to school, and Miiko went off to her mother's place.

With her legs chained, Piiko couldn't go very far. She often wished that just once she could climb to the top of the big chestnut tree that stood right there before her eyes. Today, as always, she was chained to the base of the chestnut tree. "If only someone would be my friend!" she thought, casting hopeful glances this way and that. Just then, she heard a great noise, a pair of huge wings flapping. What on earth could it be? She looked toward the sound. A large hawk was circling above the pond. The bird was the same shape as Piiko. She called out to it, "Pii, pii! Here I am! Here I am! Come play with me!"

The large hawk took no notice and continued to circle the pond. Suddenly it dived and snatched a carp from the pond, then flew swiftly away. None of the family was home. Piiko knew that the family were very fond of the carp. "Give it back! Give it back!" she cried, trying to chase after the bird and retrieve the carp. But her legs were chained; she could only flap her wings and cry "Pii! Pii!"

Several days passed. Just as Piiko was wishing that Masao would come home soon, there was another great flapping of wings. The large hawk was back for a carp.

"Please, I beg you! Don't take the carp! Father loves them. I'll save the food they give me and give it to you instead. Just for today won't you be patient and go home, please?" Piiko begged with all her heart. But the large hawk made a threatening face and screeched, "Shut up, peewee; don't bother me!" and continued to circle round and round the pond, hunting for carp.

"No! I won't shut up! There'll just be fewer and fewer carp. If the people in the house find out that the carp are disappearing, that'll make them unhappy. Please," she begged again with all her heart, "don't take any more!"

The large hawk was furious. "You make all that racket, crying 'Pii! Pii!' and now the carp have all gone down to the bottom. I can't catch anything today."

Just then the kitten Miiko pranced up. A gleam appeared in the large hawk's eyes as he turned to swoop on the kitten. "Little Miiko, look out!" Piiko shrieked. "Run away! Quick! Run away!"

Realizing that the hawk was after her, Miiko cowered in fear. I must save Miiko, Piiko thought. If ever the large hawk should get those sharp claws into her, that will be the end of her; Miiko will die. Piiko flapped her wings noisily, making a great commotion. She pulled at the chain on her leg as if her very life depended on it, and then—the chain broke in two! "I've done it!" Suddenly, with a surge of vigor, she was airborne!

"Trying to stop me, are you?" screeched the large hawk. "I'll kill you!" He swooped down to attack, and the battle began. But Piiko was just a fledgling and no match for the larger bird. Every time the large hawk's claws would strike her, five or six feathers would pull loose and flutter away in the wind. Piiko's whole body was covered with wounds, yet she fought on bravely. Her energy was exhausted; she felt she would soon fall to the ground.

Just at that moment, Masao returned home from school and saw what was happening. Immediately he took aim at the large hawk and started throwing stones. The large hawk knew he was no match for a human and flew away. Piiko, her strength spent, fluttered down at Masao's feet and didn't move. "Piiko! Come on! You can't die!" he cried as he tended her wounds. That night, when Father and Mother came in from their work in the fields, Masao told them the story. "Piiko, you may be small, but you fought bravely. Well done! Well done!" Father praised her, and he slipped a silver ring around her leg.

Several days passed, and Piiko's wounds healed completely. Piiko was no longer chained. Father told Piiko, "You're to guard the carp and the kitten." Piiko was overjoyed. Now she could fly up to the top of the chestnut tree and gaze at the beautiful scenery in the distance.

When Masao would come home from school, he would take her to the rice paddies. Before long, it was autumn and waves of golden rice swayed in the paddies. In the paddies at Piiko's house, there were no naughty sparrows who came to steal the rice. Piiko hadn't bullied the sparrows even once, but one look at Piiko was enough to send them flying off in fright. Piiko was happy. At night, she could search out the most comfortable branch to sleep on, and by day she could play wherever she liked.

And so the days passed. Piiko was on the top of the chestnut tree, waiting anxiously for Masao to come home from school, when she heard a familiar flap of wings. The large hawk was approaching. As soon as he spotted Piiko he said, "Today I've come to tell you something," and flew down to land beside her.

"Get this, peewee! I'm not here to catch carp today, I've come to take you away with me. I told the others how you got the best of me the other day, and they were all for ganging up on you and getting even; but the Great King told me that I should fetch you first, so here I am. You're to come with me now to the third mountain."

Piiko was certain the big hawk would do something dreadful to her again, and she refused to go. "My wings are weak; I can't possibly fly all the way to the third mountain."

"What? You can't fly? Don't give me that stuff!" he bellowed ferociously. "You'll come with me, or I'll be back with the whole gang; and we'll catch every last carp in the pond!" Piiko knew that the family would be heartbroken if all the carp were caught, and she would have failed in her duty. She plucked up her courage and decided to go.

The third mountain was a long, long way away. By the time they were halfway there, Piiko was completely exhausted, but summoning all her strength, she flew on. When they got to the third mountain, she was amazed. What a huge flock of hawks were gathered there, awaiting her arrival!

Piiko was brought before the Great King. The Great King fixed his fearsome glaring gaze upon her. "So you're the peewee who takes the side of humans, are you?" he demanded, in a voice so loud it resounded through the forest.

"Yes, that's me."

"Why do you take the side of our enemies?"

"Because I was brought up by people. They're my parents. They're not my enemies," Piiko answered bravely and with conviction.

"Don't you realize? Your real parents weren't humans. They were hawks. Humans shot and killed your real parents. You were captured alive by the enemies of your parents. From now on, you'll live here with us. And you'll take revenge on people."

"But I'm indebted to humans for bringing me up. You say that humans killed my real parents, but it wasn't Father or Mother who did that. I was very young then, but I still remember. I was so hungry I thought I'd die. My father left the nest early in the morning to look for food. We waited and waited, but he never came back. It was snowing that day. When he still hadn't returned by evening, my mother went out to look for him. And even after it got dark, my mother didn't come back. I was shivering with cold, and so famished I was crying. Whenever it was cold, my mother would warm me up under her wing; but now, all by myself, I was so lonely and scared I couldn't bear it. When it got dark, I couldn't see anything, and I didn't know what to do. But I decided I'd go and look for my mother anyhow. I flew frantically around and around the area, because I was so sad I couldn't stay still. I crashed into branches and fell to the ground, any number of times. Even so, I'd pull myself up again and fly recklessly around in circles. After a while I sensed that I'd come to an open space, because I'd stretch out my wings and they didn't hit anything anymore. Then, in the distance, I could faintly make out a light. I made for it with all my strength. I was so intent on reaching it that I don't know how long it took. I felt that if I could just make it to the light, I'd find my mother. But before I could reach the light, I fell to the ground, famished and exhausted. I don't know what happened after that. When I came to, I was cuddled up on a warm human lap. At first I was afraid, but then I realized that the human wouldn't do me any harm. My present Father isn't a hunter; it was someone else who had killed my real parents. At first, I wanted to return to the nest in the mountains, and I tried to escape; but when I thought carefully about it, I realized that I'd be repaying a debt with in-gratitude. They saved my life when I was on the point of death, and they brought me up—that was genuine kindness on the part of the people at my new home. And they're very fond of the carp in the pond, and the kitten, too. They'd be terribly sad if all of them were taken away. You say that humans are bad, but not all of them are bad. Please, I beg you, at least don't take anything from the people at my house. If there's anything at all I can do for you, just ask for it. And if you can't grant my request, then kill me, please, here and now. To see those people at home made sad would be more than I could bear." In a flood of tears she made her plea.

The Great King was crying, too. "Very well. In deference to the purity of your motives, I promise that we shall no longer take from the people of your home. No objections, anyone?" the king inquired.

"Indeed, Great King," they assented. "In deference to Little Piiko's kindness, we shall do nothing whatever that might make her sad."

The sun was setting, and there in the middle of the forest it grew dark. Piiko prepared to leave, but the others tried to stop her. "The sun's about to set; just for tonight stay here in the for-est and go home early tomorrow morning."

"If I hurry, I can make it back before dark," she said, as she took leave of everyone and hurried off to the home where her human parents would be waiting. Piiko was utterly exhausted. She wanted to fly home from the third mountain without stopping, but try as she might, her strength was fading. Just one more broad expanse and she'd be over the fields of her home. The familiar chestnut tree came faintly into view. The sun disappeared behind the mountain, and the sky glowed fiery red. "Oh how tired I am! I'll just rest here a bit," she thought, and she perched on a pine tree to rest her wings.

A lone hunter lay in wait for just such a moment, but Piiko was thinking only of home and didn't notice. The hunter took aim and pulled the trigger. Crack! The same instant that she heard the shot ring out, Piiko felt a burning pain in her stomach. Blood gushed from the wound. In a desperate effort to make it home she tried to take off, but all she could do was flap her wings helplessly as she fell to the ground.

"Gotcha!" The hunter was delighted and picked her up. And then it happened. The silver ring around her leg caught the last rays of sunset and sparkled in the light. "What's this?" The hunter examined it. On the ring were written the words "Piiko, aged one year." "Damn! Don't tell me this was someone's pet hawk! What have I done? If only I'd kept calm and looked a bit more carefully; surely I'd have noticed the ring on its leg! But when I saw it was a hawk, I got too excited. I shouldn't have shot down just any hawk I happened to see. I'm so sorry! Forgive me, please!" He did apologize, but Piiko could not hear his voice. Cradled in the hunter's arms, she thought that Father held her in his arms. "Father, I've good news! I got them to promise they wouldn't catch Little Miiko or the carp!" That was what she intended to say, but a faint cry, "Pii! Pii!" was all that could be heard as sweet little Piiko's spirit rose up to join the spirits of her real mother and father in heaven.

At all times and in all things, we humans tend to judge the worth of something by its outward appearance only. But even a bad person may have a good heart. We should look carefully into one another's hearts and do what we can to help one another.

Adults may laugh when they read this and think it terribly childish; but the children were quite taken with it. They listened so intently—"And then? And then?"—and wouldn't let me go. Watching their innocent smiling faces, all painful thoughts would disappear from my mind. I hadn't even been to primary school, but here was something I could do! Being in love isn't the only way of loving. I realized with all my being that if you loved somebody—it didn't matter who it was—and dedicated yourself to bringing joy to your loved one, you, too, would be redeemed.

Whether I saw a dog or a flower, I was always on the lookout for something I could turn into a story. I no longer had any spare time to brood over unimportant things.

VAIN DREAMS

"Auntie! Auntie!" the children would say as they wound their soft, smooth arms around my neck. There are no words to describe how good it felt. I couldn't help but be ashamed of myself, the way I'd carried on so disgracefully, doing any damned thing I felt like. But my heart was cleansed by the children's embrace, and I gave up drinking and sleeping around once and for all.

When I think how wildly I behaved between the time I arrived here and the autumn of last year, it was extraordinary. When I'd see one of the town's notables sitting at the head of the table and lording it over everyone in the room, I'd feel driven to do something nasty to knock the wind out of his sails. Or if a geisha who was in debt would say to me, even jokingly, "Elder Sister, I'm so in love with that man I think I might run away with him!" I'd egg her on— "Yes, yes, do run away!"—and show her how to arrange it; then I'd gloat to myself as I listened to them bemoan their losses at the geisha house. More than once I did that!

I also played this trick one day on a disheveled woman who burst into the restaurant weeping. "Is my husband here?" she says. "He's run off with all our money and hasn't been home for three days."

"Is it the money you're looking for?" I asked her nastily. "Or are you chasing after your husband?"

"There's no money at home to buy rice," she sobbed. "And when the rice's gone, how are we going to live? There'll be nothing to feed the children!"

"So, it's money you're after, then. No wonder your husband's cheating on you when that's all you think about! I'd have a mind to tell you if I found anything out, but I can't stomach the way you talk. If you've got nothing better to do than run around crying like a madwoman, why don't you air your bedding instead, so it doesn't stink of piss? Let that old man of yours sleep on a bed that smells like sunshine for a change! Sunshine's free, you know!"

"Do you know where he is? Tell me, please! I'll be forever in your debt."

"You think *I* know? Don't be such an idiot! Go on home and wash your face!"

I threw her out, but then I went out myself to try and track her down. When I caught up with her, I said, "Don't panic! Money comes and money goes; your turn will come." I tried to buck up her hopes and then paid her to run any errand I could think of until I was broke.

It got to the point that I was known as the big blockhead of Toyoshina. But in playing with the children, I gradually began to gain some peace of mind. A child's heart is a blank sheet. Should the children retain any memory of my present existence when they grew up, it would be the indelible image of that old whore that would remain. But it wasn't too late to change. I resolved that so long as even one child was prepared to come to me and wrap its arms around my neck, I would do nothing sluttish, and that until the day the flame of my life burned out, I'd make up nice children's stories to warm at least one heart. These humble ambitions sustained me.

Day by day, children grow up. Children who had played with me only yesterday would run away when they'd see me today. Perhaps it was because I worked at a restaurant, or perhaps they'd heard something about me from someone, but it didn't upset me, nor did it cause me to lose heart.

I began to think about giving up work that involved keeping company with drunken customers and taking a job that would be of more direct benefit to the world. When I inquired at the welfare section of the prefectural office, they told me that if I were to sign up with the Matsumoto Vocational Guidance Bureau, I'd be able to learn a trade that suited me better; so I went to see them. But nowadays there's a national examination even to become a hairdresser or a barber; so of course there's an exam to get into the Vocational Guidance Bureau! And to pass it, you need to be educated at least to the level of a prewar girls' school or the new postwar junior high school. People with no education would have to get a book called the *Official Syllabus* and bring themselves up to that level of knowledge, I was told. I was shocked and disappointed.

Then I thought I might learn how to sew and work from home, but when I looked into that, I found out that you had to provide your own materials, which with one thing and another would cost about 10,000 yen a month. There was no way I could come up with that kind of money. What about becoming an assistant at a kindergarten? This was my last hope. I had them make inquiries for me, but although they didn't come right out and say that someone of my background was "unsuitable," I was turned down with words to that effect.

I'd tried everything. Just when I'd begun to feel something like a human being, it turned out to be too late. I might not like being a waitress in a restaurant, but no one else was going to feed me. Nor was I the only one struggling. To live an ordinary life, like any ordinary person, must have been the vain dream of countless others.

THE PROSTITUTION PREVENTION ACT

Working as I did as a waitress in a restaurant, I was constantly reminded just how gullible women could be.

One woman would set up house with someone, then they'd split up and she'd be left flat broke, with nothing to wear even, and she'd come back to work in the restaurant. Three or four times she did this, but she seemed never to learn. Someone would come on to her a bit sweetly, she'd go all ga-ga and set up house with him; then, six months or a year later, she'd be back, working as a geisha again.

"You're back again? If you don't straighten up and get a grip on yourself, you'll come to grief in the end," someone would warn her.

"I don't go into it intending to break up. This time I meant it to be for keeps, I really tried my best; but when there's nothing left to sell and we've run out of money, we split up," she'd say resignedly. "Still, I was able to live the life of a normal person for a whole year, and if the price of that is ending up without a stitch of clothing, I've no regrets!" Yet even though the price of that year of easy living was two or three more years of work, as soon as she'd cleared her debts and had a few kimono of her own, once again, with never a thought for the consequences, she'd throw herself on the mercy of some man who, it seemed to me, simply wasn't worth it.

That reminds me of another woman: "Whenever I take customers I'm always careful to use something, but I was giving him special treatment. And then he says he's caught a disease from me and he's demanding compensation. I tell him it couldn't possibly have been me, but he won't listen. And then he comes to the geisha house to negotiate, can you believe it? I'm absolutely certain I had no disease; but even if he had caught something from me, you'd think that if he really loved me he'd want to keep it quiet, right? I was so in love with that man! When I found out he'd been having me on, I was so mad I got a carving knife from the kitchen and tried to stab him, but I couldn't do it; and what with compensation money and all, it cost me 50,000 yen, and I couldn't stay there anymore. I realize now that I've ended up in this fix because I'm a professional woman; so I'm going to save up all my money, and after I've got a place that's all my own, then I'll fall in love for real."

It was around that time that I first heard the words "prostitution prohibition ordinance"[2] and "social welfare" on the radio, and the sense of calm that I thought I'd achieved was again disturbed. Prostitution isn't something that will simply disappear just because you've passed a law against it. Probably this stems from a well-meaning attempt to rescue these women from exploitation and profiteering at the hands of rapacious entrepreneurs; but among those making the laws, were there any women like us, who couldn't have survived if they hadn't prostituted themselves? I went to see a newsreel. Those women legislators, all done up in their finery, mincing about so proudly on their tour of the red-light district—they were just having fun, I was forced to conclude. If they thought all that goggle-eyed gawking was going to help them understand what goes on in the whorehouses, they were very badly mistaken.

In this town, too, there's an officially designated red-light district;[3] but even if prostitution is prohibited, those women will have nowhere else to go; they're at their wit's end. Some people in the business say that all they'll have to do is turn their houses into inns and have their women work as maids.

The reality is that where I live, the number of geisha has increased. If a geisha or a maid sleeps with a customer and gets paid, isn't that prostitution? But if they're accused, they'll just say they're in love with each other. There's no way you can pass a law against being in love! Nobody becomes a prostitute because she enjoys it.

It's human instinct, is it not, to fill your belly when you're hungry, even if you have to steal to do it? Just passing laws banning prostitution isn't going to accomplish anything.

On nights when this problem has me all worked up, I have a dream that goes like this: There's a large house that looks like a school. People who have nowhere to go, and people who are out of work gather there. These women do the work they're fitted for. There are some geisha. And the waitresses, the women who work in bars—all those who labor away from the house pay a fixed amount per month for board and lodging. There are also people who cook, people who do the washing, and people who sew. These people who work at the house all receive something. And everyone contributes 100 yen a month, which builds into a fund that is used if anyone is sick. I'm sure there are other people who have dreams like this—people who are crying over misfortunes worse than mine, people who are drifting about helplessly.

"Do you know of any place that's looking for help?" Whenever I hear people who are drifting from place to place say that, I realize just how fortunate I still am. I've got a place to work and children to dream of playing with. When the lotus flowers bloom, I sing nonsense songs called *mambo* and go dancing through the rice paddies with the children. "The lotuses have bloomed! The lotuses have bloomed! Come all! Come all! Let's dance!" When I happen to hear some children I pass singing snatches of that silly song I taught them, I feel so full of joy I could cry.

CATS' PAWS

Last winter, about six o'clock on a morning when there'd been a heavy frost, they said a baby had been abandoned, so I went to have a look. It was a little boy about six months old; cradled in the policeman's arms, he was smiling. For some reason my face turned bright red, and my armpits felt drenched with sweat. That child, I was certain, was smiling at me, quite unconsciously. As tiny as he was, he was trying to curry favor with others. Cradled in the arms of a stranger, someone he'd never seen before, he wasn't crying, he was radiating charm. That's how it seemed to me. How was he ever to amount to anything? What sort of person was he to become? Could he ever be as happy as ordinary folk?

If you kill someone, that's a crime; yet abandoning a child isn't a terribly serious offense. Laws, as we call them, are the creation of humans, are they not? So why don't they make laws that punish child abandonment more severely? I was assailed by a sudden desire to grab hold of that child and wring his neck. I wanted him to vanish from this world while he still knew nothing, and the effort of restraining myself made me sweat. I told people that if the child were mine, that's what I'd do.

"Oh Sayo-san, you and your sermons against childbearing again!" they laughed; but in this society, has there ever been an abandoned child who's ever gone on to be as happy as other people? There may be exceptions, but I'm sure that most go through life lurking in the shadows, living in fear and trembling, embittered because the world has treated them unfairly.

"Never give birth to children thoughtlessly!" I want to shout it out loud. That is why, stroke by faltering stroke, I've written all this down. The horrid treatment meted out to me at the landlord's place, the fate awaiting me when I was sold. . . . Only when I turned thirty did I finally feel for the first time that I was free, that I could live as I liked, as an individual. It's as if at thirty, I'd been born for the first time. Until then, I was never anything more than someone's tool.

But it's too late. I despair of nothing, yet neither have I any hopes. I'm the person who's told she can't even be employed as a kindergarten assistant. Sure, I'll find bits and pieces of work to keep me going; but who knows when those jobs will dry up and I won't be able to carry on? Yet despite all, I've found peace of mind. Gradually, I've been learning how to resign myself to these things. At the end of last year and over New Year's, my liver was acting up again, and I spent some time lying quietly in bed; I thought up some children's stories, and I wrote an account of my past life.[4]

And then in May of this year I heard that farmers around here were so short of help for rice planting that they "wanted to borrow the cat's paws," as the saying goes. My hands would do as well as cats' paws, I figured, and I got myself ready to go out and help. "I'll lend you a pair of cat's paws!"

"Don't be ridiculous! This work's too much for you, Sayo-san!" The farmers were aghast; but taking no notice whatsoever, I marched into the paddy. I was determined that if others could do it, then so could I. Not on my life was anyone going to get the better of me!

Come evening, they told me they'd pay me 350 yen a day; and would I please come back tomorrow. Three hundred and fifty yen? Not bad at all. My luck had turned. The next morning, I got up again at six o'clock and went off to work. People were shocked to see me planting rice. "Sayo-san! What on earth are you up to?" they teased me. "You trying to kill yourself or something?"

"I'm as strong as a goblin's grandchild," I retorted. "There's nothing I can't do!" But not a single passerby could resist calling out to tease me. Well, shit, this is a pain; there must be something I can say that'll shut them up once and for all. I decided I'd respond with this:

"Nothing's impossible when you put your mind to it! A woman like me, I could steal someone's husband away if I put my mind to it!"

"No doubt about it!" someone says, and then another guy chimes in, "Wish you'd steal me away!" and we all had a big laugh.

Once the rice planting was finished, I got a job minding children. As it happened, I'd occasionally been looking after the children of the couple who ran the candy shop, and they asked me, partly just to be kind, to mind their two children aged three and one. I was delighted that this unexpected good fortune had come my way. No longer would I have to charm and cajole drunken customers to make a living.

"How about that, Masaru? Things turned out pretty well, didn't they? Your sister can live a respectable life. You of all people should be happy to hear that, I reckon."

It's a simple pleasure, I guess; but for me, being able to speak to a photograph of my little brother without the slightest sense of guilt is the greatest of all joys.

Masuda Sayo's "secret place," the zelkova tree with the sloping trunk that she used to climb in order to hide in its thick foliage.

The geisha registry office in Suwa.

"Ōte Registry," the sign at the entrance to the geisha registry office.

The Inari Shrine by the station, where Masuda went daily to pray for a miscarriage.

The present-day geisha
district in Suwa:
(right) in the foreground
is the gate to a restaurant
of the sort to which
Masuda was called to
entertain; (below) a
street lined with the bars
and nightclubs that
have replaced older-style
establishments.

Afterword

Masuda Sayo is still alive. Her memoir *Geisha*, written and published in 1957 when she was thirty-two years old, became a "long-
seller" and remains in print. It has also been adapted for radio
and television. I had hoped to meet Masuda and interview her:
how, I wondered, had the writing and successful publication of
her autobiography affected her life afterward? But my request
was politely declined by her editor, Oda Mitsuki, who informed
me that "Masuda-san does not meet people who know about her
past, nor people who want to know about it." His letter of December 4, 2000, continued:

> She is now an old woman of seventy-five; more than forty years
> have passed since her days as a geisha. At long last she has found
> release from her past suffering and achieved a way of life that is
> normal and tranquil. Those around her now are people who

know nothing of her past. I myself have not met with her for more than thirty years. Please, leave her in peace.

Let me add, moreover, that the wounds Masuda-san suffered as a result of publishing her book were far from insignificant. In the country town where she lived, even though no one there had even read the book, people concocted a scandal out of what little they'd heard of the story, and in the end, the flood of rumors forced her to leave town. This was something for which I too, as her publisher, felt a heavy responsibility. I came to think of guarding Masuda-san's privacy as my principal obligation, and I still think so today.

It seems only fair to respect both Masuda's wish not to be disturbed and her editor's obligation to guard her privacy. When approached for permission to translate her memoir, Masuda conveyed to me through her publisher the wish that I translate her words into English "as truthfully as possible." This I have endeavored to do. When Columbia University Press undertook to publish this translation, Masuda reiterated her determination to continue her quiet life and her desire that she "not become famous."

Tokyo, June 2002

Notes

1. For readers who wish to know more about geisha, their origins, their history, and the nature of their unique society, as well as the routines of their everyday lives, there is no better resource than Liza Crihfield Dalby's *Geisha*. Other useful accounts include Jodi Cobb's photographic essay *Geisha: The Life, the Voices, the Art*; Eleanor Underwood's miscellany *The Life of a Geisha*; and Lesley Downer's *Geisha: The Secret History of a Vanishing World*. Both Dalby and Downer contrast hot-springs-resort geisha with their more refined sisters in the city and allow readers to hear something of how contemporary hot-springs geisha see their lives.

Snow Country (*Yukiguni*), the famous novel by Kawabata Yasunari (1899–1972), is set at the Yuzawa hot spring in Niigata Prefecture in the 1930s. Although its principal concern is the psychology of the male protagonist Shimamura, a regular customer of the geisha Komako, the novel contains a surprising number of references to the contractual arrangements made by country geisha. As Edward G. Seidensticker, translator of *Snow Country*, remarks in his introduction: "If the hot-spring geisha is not a social outcast, she is perilously near being one. The city geisha may become a celebrated musician or dancer, a political intriguer, even a dispenser of patronage. The hot-spring geisha must go on entertaining week-end guests, and the pretense that she is an artist and not a prostitute is often a thin one indeed" (p. vi).

2. The figures for Japanese emigration to Manchuria, arranged according to prefecture, may be found in Takahashi Yasutaka, *Shōwa senzenki no nōson to Manshū imin*, pp. 118–19, 152. My thanks to Anke Scherer of Ruhr-University Bochum for directing me to this study.

3. Suwa, where Masuda lived and worked as a geisha, was, in the Edo period (1615–1867), the castle town of the Takashima domain, seat of the Suwa house. The town of Suwa was divided into Upper and Lower Suwa (Kami-no-Suwa and Shimo-no-Suwa); they were the last two post towns (*shukuba*) on the Kai High Road (Kōshū kaidō), a public high road that ran west from Edo (present-day Tokyo) to Lower Suwa. At Lower Suwa, the Kai High Road met the Middle Mountain Road (Nakasendō), the inland route from Kyoto to Edo. The first stop on the Middle Mountain Road beyond Lower Suwa was Shiojiri, the town closest to the village where Masuda was born.

4. The geisha whom Kawabata used as his model for the character Komako went by the professional name Matsue. For photographs of Matsue (b. 1915) and a brief account of her life, see Hirayama Mitsuo, "Echigo-Yuzawa to *Yukiguni*," pp. 5, 59–60. For an attempt to read *Snow Country* from Komako's perspective, see Tajima Yoko, "A Rereading of *Snow Country* from Komako's Point of View."

5. At the very end of her memoir, Masuda writes that in May 1957 she was paid 350 yen a day working as a farmhand. Assuming that she worked twenty-five days a month, this amounts to a monthly income of 8,750 yen, a little more than the average earned by women working in the construction industry (272 yen a day) and a little less than women working in "pink-collar" occupations such as telephone opera-

tor (10,094 yen a month) and nurse (11,985 yen a month). These figures are from *Kanketsu Shōwa kokusei sōran*, vol. 3, table 14-35, p. 62, table 14-34, pp. 59, 61.

6. I have borrowed my description of Masuda's natural style from Tim Parks's description, in "A Chorus of Cruelty" (p. 140), of the style of Giovanni Verga's (1840–1922) Sicilian novellas, such as *I Malavoglia* (1889; translated by Judith Landry as *The House by the Medlar Tree*, 1985).

7. Oda Mitsuki was working as an editor at the Heibonsha publishing house when he was assigned to prepare Masuda's memoir for publication. His account of their working relationship is contained in "Ikiru chikara to bun no chikara" (The Power of Living and the Power of Writing), his afterword to the revised version of Masuda's memoir, *Geisha: Kutō no hanshōgai*, pp. 228–29.

8. The Prostitution Prevention Act (Baishun bōshi hō) passed the Japanese Diet on May 24, 1956, as Law no. 118 of 1956 and went into effect on April 1, 1957, although its penal provisions did not take effect until one year later, on April 1, 1958. Article 3 of the act states, "No person shall commit prostitution or be the client of a prostitute," but no punishment is specified for prostitution per se; punishment is specified only for acts such as public solicitation, procurement, forced (or the attempt to force) prostitution, offering or receiving compensation for another's prostitution, and the provision or management of a place for prostitution. For an abbreviated English translation of the act, see Baishun taisaku shingikai, ed., *Baishun taisaku no genkyō*, pp. 518–29. For English-language studies of prostitution in the postwar period, see Shiga-Fujime Yuki, "The Prostitutes' Union and the Impact of the 1956 Anti-Prostitution Law in Japan"; Sheldon Garon, *Molding Japanese Minds: The State in Everyday Life*, pp. 195–205; John W. Dower, *Embracing Defeat: Japan in the Wake of World War II*, pp. 122–39; Michael S. Molasky, *The American Occupation of Japan and Okinawa: Literature and Memory*, pp. 103–29; and G. G. Rowley, "Prostitutes Against the Prostitution Prevention Act."

9. Takeo Shizuko's estimate of how much Yoshiwara prostitutes earned per month is found in the roundtable discussion printed in "Kōsei e no tatakai," p. 1.

10. Yamamoto Hirofumi points out in his essay "Tōshindai no jo-seishi" (Life-Size Women's History) that in Edo-period Japan, "all women of whatever rank were at risk of having to turn to prostitution. If a husband lost his job, even the wife of a samurai might soon fall upon such hard times that she had no option but to sell herself" (p. 225). Although Yamamoto uses the common expression *mi o uru* (to sell oneself), the arrangement referred to by this locution was actually an indenture contract, by which a person agreed to work for a certain number of years in return for an initial payment—in effect, a loan against future earnings—that was typically paid to a member of the in-dentured person's family.

11. In October 1872, the Meiji Council of State reaffirmed the ban on human trafficking when it issued the Ordinance Liberating Prosti-tutes (Shōgi kaihō rei). On the *Maria Luz* trial, which led to the issu-ing of the ordinance, see Garon, *Molding Japanese Minds*, pp. 91–92; and Peter F. Kornicki's introduction to *Collected Works of Frederick Vic-tor Dickins*, vol. 1, pp. xviii–xxi. For an English translation of the ordi-nance, see J. E. De Becker, *The Nightless City or, The "History of the Yoshi-wara Yūkwaku,"* pp. 91–92; and Cecilia Segawa Seigle, *Yoshiwara: The Glittering World of the Japanese Courtesan*, pp. 221–22.

12. For an account of the nature and use of such indenture contracts in prewar Japan, see J. Mark Ramseyer, "Indentured Prostitution in Im-perial Japan: Credible Commitments in the Commercial Sex Industry," revised as "Promissory Credibility: Sex." Ramseyer's use of rational-choice theory in these essays attributes to women who worked in the sexual services industry a degree of personal autonomy, or "resourceful-ness" ("Promissory Credibility," p. 134), not recognized in other ac-counts. Masuda's experiences also reveal the limits of this approach: she was not a signatory to her indenture contract, if indeed such a document existed; and although she learned to make the most of her situation ("ad-vance her private best interests," p. 134), notions such as "to contract to work," "demand and receive," and "expected earnings" (all p. 121) were completely foreign to her and the other geisha she recalls in her memoir.

13. Retail rice prices are listed in *Nedanshi nenpyō: Meiji, Taishō, Shōwa*, p. 161. In premodern Japan, 1 *koku*, or about 150 kilograms, of

unpolished rice was the rough measure of the amount required to feed one adult male for one year.

14. The classic depiction of rural poverty in the early years of the twentieth century is Nagatsuka Takashi's (1879–1915) novel *The Soil* (*Tsuchi*), published in 1910. As Ann Waswo, translator of *The Soil: A Portrait of Rural Life in Meiji Japan*, suggests in her preface, the novel is also "an informal ethnography of a rural community and its inhabitants" (p. vii).

15. In "Ikiru chikara to bun no chikara," Oda recalls "pestering Masuda-san with questions about her sexual initiation" (p. 230). Masuda's account of the routine nature of sex for payment ("points") in her world is confirmed by a 1928 survey calculating that almost 80 percent of geisha in Tokyo performed sexual services for money with customers they had never seen before (*mizuten de ari shokugyōteki ni warai o uru*). See Kusama Yaso'o, *Jokyū to baishōfu*, p. 20.

16. In the Edo-period licensed quarters, where geisha originated, "art" (*gei*, that is, dancing, singing, and so forth) was used to enhance not only the sex itself but also the profits to be made from selling sex, for sex was (merely) the "climax" of a long day or evening spent in the company of entertainers, all of whom had to be paid. In the modern era, however, the art of the geisha, however intimately related to sex it may remain in the workplace of the geisha, tends to be presented to the outside world as "art" performed purely for its own sake and in no way related to sex. The connection between the two has been deliberately obscured, one result of which is that many writers either emphasize unduly the geisha's artistic accomplishments or deny her sexual duties, or both. See, for example, T. Fujimoto, *The Story of the Geisha Girl*, pp. vii–viii, 2–3; Kikou Yamata, *Three Geishas*, p. 9; Underwood, *Life of a Geisha*, pp. 10, 51; and Mineko Iwasaki, *Geisha, a Life*. Dedication to traditional arts is also stressed in several recent popular accounts of geisha in Japan, such as *Vogue Nippon*, September 1999, pp. 196–97; and *Tōkyōjin*, June 2000, a special issue devoted to geisha.

17. Mayumi is one of Cobb's informants, quoted in *Geisha*, p. 112.

18. Nishiyama Matsunosuke recognizes that despite the hardships of their daily lives, women's mastery of traditional arts could enable

them "to live as the subjects of their own lives" (*Kuruwa* [1963], cited in Yamamoto, "Tōshindai no joseishi," p. 214). This point is also suggested by Sone Hiromi, "Conceptions of Geisha: A Case Study of the City of Miyazu," especially pp. 232–33.

1. A Little Dog, Abandoned and Terrified

1. Mariko Asano Tamanoi's *Under the Shadow of Nationalism: Politics and Poetics of Rural Japanese Women* contains a valuable chapter on nursemaids. She points out that the essential characteristic of *komori* was that they were the daughters of poor families: "Unlike European nursemaids and nannies, *komori* were not status symbols but, rather, an economic necessity for the employers, whose own labors left them no time to devote to child rearing. Furthermore, *komori* were not sheltered in the homes of their employers; forming small groups, they spent most of their days with their charges in 'public' places such as shrine compounds, playgrounds, river banks, or simply the streets" (p. 56).

Tamanoi illustrates her account with a beautiful photograph of a group of *komori*, some only slightly larger than the babies strapped to their backs, taken by the French journalist Félicien Challaye and originally published in his *Le Japon illustré*, p. 55. See also *Shashin de miru 100 nen mae no Nihon*, vol. 1, [p. 3], p. 17.

2. Indentured servitude as farmworkers was a common experience for rural children in other countries as well, of course. In prewar England, at labor markets like those described in Thomas Hardy's novels, children were indentured for periods of six months to a year. Typically they were not paid until they had served the full term of their contract; and if they left early for any reason, they went unpaid. Several such childhoods are recalled in the oral history compiled by Steve Humphries and Beverley Hopwood, *Green and Pleasant Land*.

2. The Sunburned Novice

1. The Palace of the Dragon King (*ryūgū*) and his daughter Princess Oto (*oto hime*) appear in the Japanese fairy tale "Urashima Tarō." Urashima is a fisherman's son who is transported on the back of a turtle to the Dragon King's palace beneath the sea. There he falls in love

with Princess Oto and lives happily for three years before deciding to return to his aged parents at home. When he arrives back on land, he finds that everything has changed: three hundred years have passed while he has been away. He opens the box inlaid with mother-of-pearl that Princess Oto gave to him when they parted, ignoring her command not to do so. The instant he does, white smoke wafts up and he suddenly begins to age. His hair turns white, his eyes dim, his body grows cold, and then he dies.

2. Masuda's description of the violence she endured as part of her training in the geisha arts is painful to read, but physical chastisement is a concomitant of any artistic training in Japan when that training is for a professional purpose and not as a polite accomplishment. I thank Brian Powell of the University of Oxford for pointing this out to me. Masuda herself seems to realize this when she observes, "If they were teaching a young lady of means, I was sure, they wouldn't treat her this way, even if she did make a mistake."

3. Relationships among residents of a geisha house are modeled on familial relationships. Thus Masuda calls the woman who runs her house "Mother" (Okāsan); the woman's husband, "Father" (Otōsan); and the older geisha in her house, either "Elder Sister" (Onēsan) or a combination of their professional names plus "elder sister," producing Takechiyo-nēsan, Shizuka-nēsan, and so on. Even after they leave the profession, geisha continue to address one another by these familial designations: to Masuda, Karuta will always be Karuta-nēsan. As the youngest in her house, Masuda was called by a variety of names, as she explains. The most affectionate of these was a combination of her nickname Tsuru (Crane), plus the diminutive honorific -chan, making Tsuru-chan, Little Crane. Masuda becomes an "elder sister" only when another young woman joins the house. To the new arrival, Masuda is Tsuru-nēsan, Elder Sister Crane. When Masuda becomes a fully fledged geisha, she goes by the professional name Tsuruyo, literally "Age of Cranes," an auspicious designation because cranes are thought to be long-lived.

4. Zenigata Heiji is the hero of a series of historical detective stories and novels by Nomura Kodō (1882–1963). In a total of 383 tales written

between 1931 and 1957, Kodō created the character Heiji, an *okappiki*, the lowest-ranking member of the law-enforcement hierarchy of the Edo period. His distinguishing characteristic is his ability to stop the villain in his tracks with a copper coin (*zeni*) hurled with unfailing accuracy. That he is eternally thirty-one years old and still in love with his wife, O-Shizu, an ever-youthful twenty-three, is perhaps one of the reasons why Masuda's Elder Sister Shizuka was so fond of him. The stories remain popular in contemporary Japan and are regularly revived as television dramas. For more information, see the entry for Nomura Kodō in *Nihon kindai bungaku daijiten*, vol. 3, pp. 41–42.

5. It is, of course, impossible to calculate what 100 yen might have been worth to the parents of the young woman who, as Masuda and her geisha sisters heard, had been rolled up in a mattress and suffocated at another geisha house. In 1939, male day laborers earned, on average, just under 2 yen per day, and female farmworkers earned just over 1 yen per day. For people at this level of Japanese society, then, 100 yen perhaps represented the most they could hope to earn in two or three months of uninterrupted work. These figures are from *Kanketsu Shōwa kokusei sōran*, vol. 3, table 14-11, p. 66.

6. The man on the same hospital ward as Masuda had had his foot crushed in the Suwa Pillar Festival, held every seven years in Suwa. During the festival, the trunks of sixteen cryptomeria (*sugi*) trees are hauled down the surrounding mountains and through the streets of Upper and Lower Suwa before being erected at the Great Shrine of Suwa. For a fascinating cultural history of the festival, see Elaine Gerbert, "The Suwa Pillar Festival Revisited."

3. MISS LOW GETS WISE

1. For a comprehensive account of the history and culture of kimono, readers can again turn to Liza Crihfield Dalby for the best English-language work on the subject, *Kimono: Fashioning Culture*. On geisha and kimono, see especially pp. 55, 323–35.

2. "Shallow River" is a *dodoitsu*, a short, bawdy song and dance performed to the accompaniment of a shamisen. The genre is named after the musician and comedian Dodoitsubō Senka (1796–1852). On *dodoi-*

tsu, see Liza Crihfield Dalby, *Geisha*, pp. 150, 320 n.5, 330. Dalby has also translated a collection of the more romantic songs that geisha perform in *Little Songs of the Geisha: Traditional Japanese Ko-uta*.

3. Saigō Takamori (1827–1877) was a famous statesman and general of the Meiji period (1868–1912).

4. BIRD IN A CAGE

1. The practice of *mizuage* has a parallel in the world of popular theater (*taishū engeki*), in which the virginity of male actors is bought by older women patrons in a practice known as *fude-oroshi*, literally "to use a writing brush for the first time." My thanks again to Brian Powell of the University of Oxford for this information.

2. The Shibata Circus, founded in May 1922, was one of many circuses that toured Japan in the 1920s and 1930s. Both boys and girls were "sold" (indentured) to circuses, where they were trained from an early age in acrobatics, horse riding, juggling, and the like. Circuses disappeared during the final years of World War II, their performers conscripted and their animals shot or poisoned, but the Shibata Circus was one of twenty troupes that re-formed after the war. With the rise of other forms of entertainment, particularly television, the popularity of traveling circuses declined, and the Shibata Circus disbanded in 1963. The passage of the Child Welfare Act (Jidō fukushi hō) in December 1947 specifically outlawed the employment of children under the age of fifteen in circuses, with the result that circus performers, such as Henry Yasumatsu, born in 1920 and trained as a trapeze artist, continued to work well into their sixties. Yasumatsu recalls his life as a circus performer in an interview published in "Saakasu gei ichidai." For more on the history of circuses in Japan, see Akune Iwao, *Saakasu no rekishi: Misemono-goya kara kindai saakasu e*; Ishikawa Hiroyoshi et al., eds., *Taishū bunka jiten*, pp. 285–86; and http://plaza4.mbn.or.jp/~chansuke/circus/circus_j.html (accessed on June 2, 2002), on which the foregoing is based.

3. Nagano Prefecture was well known for its silk-reeling mills where young women, daughters of the rural poor, were hired on indenture contracts and worked long hours for low wages. See E. Patricia Tsurumi, *Factory Girls: Women in the Thread Mills of Meiji Japan*.

5. AWAKENING TO LOVE

1. A man's "Number One" (*ichigō*) is his wife, and Number Two (*nigō*), Number Three (*sangō*), and so on are his mistresses, named in order of their date of acquisition.

2. *Little Lord Fauntleroy* (1886) is a novel, and *The Little Princess* (1905) is a dramatization of the novel *Sara Crewe* (1888), all by Frances Hodgson Burnett (1849–1924). Both novels were translated into Japanese by Wakamatsu Shizuko (1864–1896), the first as *Shōkōshi* (1890–1892) and the second as *Shōkōjo* (1893). Rebecca L. Copeland's *Lost Leaves: Women Writers of Meiji Japan* includes a moving chapter on Wakamatsu's life and work: "Wakamatsu Shizuko and the Freedom of Translation."

3. "Misfortune may turn out to be a blessing in disguise" is the moral traditionally drawn from the Chinese story of Old Sai and his horse (*Ningen banji Saiō ga uma*). Old Sai laments that his horse has run away and then rejoices when it comes back, leading a much finer horse with it. Attempting to ride the new horse, Old Sai's son falls off and breaks his leg, but is thus disqualified from military service and avoids being sent away from home to fight in the war. The saying is based on a story in the *Huai-nan Tzu*, a miscellany compiled early in the second century B.C.E.

6. WANDERINGS OF A CASTAWAY

1. All of Japan's geisha districts were closed down by government order on March 5, 1944, and were officially permitted to reopen on October 25, 1945.

2. The chronology of Masuda's account is somewhat confused here. She records that her *danna* died in May 1946, that it was after his death that she went to work at the dumpling-soup diner, and that the change to the new yen and the first postwar election took place while she worked at the diner. Although both these events occurred in 1946, the change to the new yen took place in February, and the election in which women first exercised their right to vote was in April.

3. For a brief biography of Yamamura Shinjirō (1908–1964), the politician from Chiba Prefecture for whom Masuda cast her vote in the

first postwar election, see *Nihon jinmei daijiten*, vol. 7, pp. 816–17. Yamamura was elected to the House of Representatives nine times between 1946 and his death and held positions in the Yoshida and Ikeda cabinets.

4. In February 1946, the Japanese government introduced newly designed yen notes and coins "in a futile attempt to control inflation" (John W. Dower, *Embracing Defeat: Japan in the Wake of World War II*, p. 102). Because all bank deposits would be frozen and all larger denominations declared invalid until exchanged for new notes, making it difficult to survive in businesses that operated on small margins and depended on a rapid turnover, Masuda's boss was collecting the 50-sen coins and 1-yen notes.

5. *His Butler's Sister*, a 1943 Universal Studios musical starring Deanna Durbin (b. 1921), was released in Japan in 1946 under the title *Haru no jokyoku* (*Prelude to Spring*). *Mayerling*, a 1936 French film starring Danielle Darrieux (b. 1917) and Charles Boyer (1897–1978), tells the story of the tragic love between Baroness Marie Vetsera and Archduke Rudolf, son of Franz Josef of Austria-Hungary, and ends with their love suicide. Banned in Japan during the war years, the film was released in 1946 under the title *Utakata no koi* (*Brief Love*). This information is from *Amerika eiga sakuhin zenshū*, pp. 292–93; *Yōroppa eiga sakuhin zenshū*, p. 51; and Nicholas Thomas and Claire Lofting, eds., *Actors and Actresses: International Dictionary of Films and Filmmakers*, pp. 128–29, 259–61, 311–12.

7. A DREAM FOR MY LITTLE BROTHER

1. "GI whore" translates the term *panpan*, a word used to describe women who worked as prostitutes in the immediate postwar period and whose principal clientele were members of the Occupation Forces. In *Embracing Defeat: Japan in the Wake of World War II*, John W. Dower offers an unusually upbeat assessment of the *panpan*'s "embrace of the conqueror" (pp. 123–39).

2. The section on the postwar black market in Dower, *Embracing Defeat* (pp. 139–48), also provides much interesting background to Masuda's own account of her black-market dealings in this chapter of her memoir.

3. "Funerary lath" translates the Japanese *sotoba* (Sanskrit *stupa*), in this case, the provisional stupas made of long thin strips of wood on which are written a Sanskrit inscription and the posthumous name of the deceased in Chinese characters. The wood is notched and pointed to suggest the shape of the more permanent stone stupa that serves as a gravestone. Services, the merit of which accrues to the deceased, are memorialized by these laths. In some regions, it is customary to mark each of the first seven memorial services with a lath bearing the name of a different Buddha. It is the heads of the fourth—the middle one—in these series of seven laths that Masuda wishes to collect.

8. THE DEPTHS OF DESPAIR

1. For an exhaustive account of the history of tuberculosis in Japan, see William Johnston, *The Modern Epidemic: A History of Tuberculosis in Japan*. Despite the discovery of the tubercle bacillus in 1882, the notion that tuberculosis was hereditary remained widespread in both the West and Japan (p. 290), and the suicide note left by Masuda's brother suggests that he believed he had inherited the disease from his father: "My life can't be saved in any case. Father died of this disease, too." In a further cruel irony, Masuda's brother became ill with the disease just after streptomycin, "the first medicinal cure for tuberculosis" (p. 287), began to be mass-produced in Japan. Just at this time, too, public-health workers were in the process of implementing the Tuberculosis Prevention Act of 1951, which specified that the government would assume "the total cost of treatment for anybody whom tuberculosis had forced either to enter a sanatorium or to quit work" (p. 288).

2. In the aftermath of her brother's suicide, when Masuda cries, "I don't care if you rip off my arms and legs and make a Daruma doll of me," she is referring to the Indian ascetic Bodhidharma (Japanese Daruma, d. 528), who is regarded as the founder of Zen Buddhism. According to popular legend, he meditated with his face to a wall for nine years until his legs had withered away. In Japan, he is commonly represented as a roly-poly doll wearing red robes and having only a torso and a face but no arms or legs.

3. In the following section and in chapter 9, Masuda's description of her life as a maid and waitress (*jochū*), her familiarity with geisha and prostitutes, as well as the opinions of "people in the business" (*gyōsha*) suggest that the restaurant where she worked was within the town's officially designated red-light district. The English word *restaurant* does not, of course, convey all the functions fulfilled by a *ryōriya* in a red-light district. As Masuda explains in chapters 3, 4, and 5 of her memoir, restaurants provided not only party rooms (*zashiki*) but also rooms with bedding where geisha could have sex with customers. *Ryōriya* are one of the "three businesses" (*sangyō*) that make up a licensed quarter, the other two being geisha houses (*okiya*), where geisha live but do not work, and houses of assignation (*machiai*). In some quarters, known as "two-business districts" (*nigyōchi*), *machiai* have ceased to exist, and only *ryōriya* and *okiya* remain.

4. In 1954, male day laborers earned, on average, about 400 yen per day. Masuda's gift of 2,000 yen to Fusako thus represents perhaps a week's income. These figures are from *Nedanshi nenpyō: Meiji, Taishō, Shōwa*, p. 173. In the final chapter of her memoir, Masuda records that she earned only 2,000 yen per week as a maid and waitress, but this sum would have been in addition to the room and board commonly provided to restaurant staff in this period.

9. The Road Back to Life

1. Gulonic acid was used as a medicine to treat damage done to the liver by excessive alcohol consumption. My thanks to Tōgō Toshihiro of the Institute for Research in Humanities, Kyoto University, for this information.

2. "Prostitution prohibition ordinance" translates Masuda's "Baishun kinshi rei." As noted in the introduction, the antiprostitution law that was eventually passed by the Japanese Diet in May 1956 is officially known as the Baishun bōshi hō, the Prostitution Prevention Act.

3. "Officially designated red-light district" translates Masuda's *tokuingai*, one of the terms used in the postwar period to refer to specifically designated areas in which prostitution was tolerated. Another phrase for such areas was "red-line zones" (*akasen chitai*), because of the

red lines used to mark them on police maps. Brothels within *tokuingai* were officially known as *tokushu inshokuten* (special restaurants). With the enforcement of the Prostitution Prevention Act beginning on April 1, 1958, the legal status of these areas, their brothels, and the women who worked in them was abolished. Recently Kimura Satoshi attempted to record what remains of the areas in his photographic essays *Akasen ato o aruku: Kieyuku yume no machi o tazunete*.

4. The "account of [her] past life" that Masuda recalls writing "at the end of last year and over New Year's" was the first version of her memoir, "Account of the Wanderings of a Country Geisha" (Aru inaka geisha no rutenki), which was published in the February 1957 issue of *Shufu no tomo* (*Housewife's Companion*).

Bibliography

Akune Iwao. *Saakasu no rekishi: Misemono-goya kara kindai saakasu e*. Tokyo: Nishida shoten, 1977.

Amerika eiga sakuhin zenshū. Tokyo: Kinema junpōsha, 1972.

Baishun taisaku shingikai, ed. *Baishun taisaku no genkyō*. Tokyo: Ōkurashō insatsukyoku, 1959.

Challaye, Félicien. *Le Japon illustré*. Paris: Librairie Larousse, 1915.

Cobb, Jodi. *Geisha: The Life, the Voices, the Art*. Introduction by Ian Buruma. New York: Knopf, 1997.

Copeland, Rebecca L. *Lost Leaves: Women Writers of Meiji Japan*. Honolulu: University of Hawai'i Press, 2000.

Dalby, Liza Crihfield. *Geisha*. Reprint, Berkeley and Los Angeles: University of California Press, 1998.

_____. *Kimono: Fashioning Culture*. Rev. ed. Seattle: University of Washington Press, 2001.

_____, ed. *Little Songs of the Geisha: Traditional Japanese Ko-uta*. Reprint, Rutland, Vt., and Tokyo: Tuttle, 2000.

De Becker, J. E. *The Nightless City or, The "History of the Yoshiwara Yūkwaku."* 3d rev. ed. Yokohama: Nössler, 1905.

Dower, John W. *Embracing Defeat: Japan in the Wake of World War II.* New York: Norton, 1999.

Downer, Lesley. *Geisha: The Secret History of a Vanishing World.* London: Headline, 2000.

Fujimoto, T. *The Story of the Geisha Girl.* London: T. Werner Laurie, ca. 1910.

Fujin shinpū [55 nos. originally published from May 1, 1952, to July 15, 1957]. Reprint, Tokyo: Akashi shoten, 1989.

Garon, Sheldon. *Molding Japanese Minds: The State in Everyday Life.* Princeton, N.J.: Princeton University Press, 1997.

Gerbert, Elaine. "The Suwa Pillar Festival Revisited." *Harvard Journal of Asiatic Studies* 56, no. 2 (1996): 319–74.

Golden, Arthur. *Memoirs of a Geisha.* New York: Knopf, 1997.

Hida Chiho. *Shinbashi seikatsu shijūnen.* Tokyo: Gakufū shoin, 1956.

Hirayama Mitsuo. "Echigo-Yuzawa to *Yukiguni*." In *Kawabata Yasunari* Yukiguni *60 shūnen* (*Kokubungaku kaishaku to kanshō* bessatsu), edited by Hasegawa Izumi and Hirayama Mitsuo, pp. 52–66. Tokyo: Shibundō, 1998.

Humphries, Steve, and Beverley Hopwood. *Green and Pleasant Land.* London: Macmillan/Channel 4 Books, 1999.

Iwasaki, Mineko, with Rande Brown. *Geisha, a Life.* New York: Simon and Schuster/Atria, 2002.

Johnston, William. *The Modern Epidemic: A History of Tuberculosis in Japan.* Cambridge, Mass.: Council on East Asian Studies, Harvard University, 1995.

Kanketsu Shōwa kokusei sōran. 4 vols. Tokyo: Tōyō keizai shinpōsha, 1991.

Kawabata Yasunari. *Yukiguni.* Tokyo: Sōgensha, 1948.

Kimura Satoshi. *Akasen ato o aruku: Kieyuku yume no machi o tazunete.* 2 vols. Tokyo: Jiyū kokuminsha, 1998, 2002.

Kornicki, Peter F. Introduction to *Collected Works of Frederick Victor Dickins.* Vol. 1, pp. ix–xxxi. Bristol: Ganesha, 1999.

Kusama Yaso'o. *Jokyū to baishōfu.* 1930. Reprinted in *Kindai fujin mondai meicho senshū: Zokuhen*, vol. 9. Tokyo: Nihon tosho sentaa, 1982.

Masuda Sayo. "Aru inaka geisha no rutenki." *Shufu no tomo* 41, no. 2 (1957): 206–14.

_____. *Geisha*. Tokyo: Heibonsha, 1957.

_____. *Geisha: Kutō no hanshōgai*. Tokyo: Heibonsha Library, 1995.

Molasky, Michael S. *The American Occupation of Japan and Okinawa: Literature and Memory*. London: Routledge, 1999.

Nedanshi nenpyō: Meiji, Taishō, Shōwa. Edited by *Shūkan Asahi*. Tokyo: Asahi shinbunsha, 1988.

Nihon jinmei daijiten. 7 vols. Tokyo: Heibonsha, 1979.

Nihon kindai bungaku daijiten. 6 vols. Tokyo: Kōdansha, 1977–1978.

Nishiyama Matsunosuke. *Kuruwa*. 1963. Reprinted in *Nishiyama Matsunosuke chosakushū*, vol. 5, pp. 1–201. Edited by Haga Noboru et al. Tokyo: Yoshikawa kōbunkan, 1985.

Oda Mitsuki. "Ikiru chikara to bun no chikara." Afterword to *Geisha: Kutō no hanshōgai*, by Masuda Sayo, pp. 223–33. Tokyo: Heibonsha Library, 1995.

Parks, Tim. "A Chorus of Cruelty." In *Hell and Back: Selected Essays*, pp. 131–47. London: Secker and Warburg, 2001.

Ramseyer, J. Mark. "Indentured Prostitution in Imperial Japan: Credible Commitments in the Commercial Sex Industry." *Journal of Law, Economics, and Organization* 7, no. 1 (1991): 89–116.

_____. "Promissory Credibility: Sex." In *Odd Markets in Japanese History: Law and Economic Growth*, pp. 109–34. Cambridge: Cambridge University Press, 1996.

Rowley, G. G. "Prostitutes Against the Prostitution Prevention Act." *U.S.-Japan Women's Journal*, English supplement. Forthcoming.

Seidensticker, Edward G., trans. *Snow Country*, by Kawabata Yasunari. New York: Knopf, 1956.

Seigle, Cecilia Segawa. *Yoshiwara: The Glittering World of the Japanese Courtesan*. Honolulu: University of Hawai'i Press, 1993.

Shashin de miru 100 nen mae no Nihon. Vol. 1. Tokyo: Maarusha, 1996.

Shiga-Fujime Yuki. "The Prostitutes' Union and the Impact of the 1956 Anti-Prostitution Law in Japan." Translated by Beverly L. Findlay-Kaneko. *U.S.-Japan Women's Journal*, English supplement no. 5 (1993): 3–27.

Sone Hiromi. "Conceptions of Geisha: A Case Study of the City of Miyazu." Translated by Suzanne O'Brien. In *Gender and Japanese History*.Vol. 1, *Religion and Customs / The Body and Sexuality*, edited by Wakita Haruko, Anne Bouchy, and Ueno Chizuko, pp. 213–33. Osaka: Osaka University Press, 1999.

Taishū bunka jiten. Edited by Ishikawa Hiroyoshi et al. Tokyo: Kōbundō, 1991.

Tajima Yoko. "A Rereading of *Snow Country* from Komako's Point of View." Translated by Donna George Storey. *U.S.-Japan Women's Journal*, English supplement no. 4 (1993): 26–48.

Takahashi Yasutaka. *Shōwa senzenki no nōson to Manshū imin*. Tokyo: Yoshikawa kōbunkan, 1997.

Takeo Shizuko et al. "Kōsei e no tatakai." *Fujin shinpū*, July 15, 1956, pp. 1–2.

Tamanoi, Mariko Asano. *Under the Shadow of Nationalism: Politics and Poetics of Rural Japanese Women*. Honolulu: University of Hawai'i Press, 1998.

Thomas, Nicholas, and Claire Lofting, eds. *Actors and Actresses: International Dictionary of Films and Filmmakers*. Vol. 3. Detroit: St. James Press, 1992.

Tōkyōjin, June 2000.

Tsurumi, E. Patricia. *Factory Girls: Women in the Thread Mills of Meiji Japan*. Princeton, N.J.: Princeton University Press, 1990.

Underwood, Eleanor. *The Life of a Geisha*. Foreword by Liza Dalby. New York: Smithmark, 1999.

Vogue Nippon, September 1999.

Waswo, Ann, trans. *The Soil: A Portrait of Rural Life in Meiji Japan*, by Nagatsuka Takashi. Reprint, Berkeley and Los Angeles: University of California Press, 1993.

Yamamoto Hirofumi. "Tōshindai no joseishi." In *Edo o tanoshimu: Mitamura Engyo no seikai*, pp. 212–26. Tokyo: Chūō kōronsha, 1997.

Yamata, Kikou. *Three Geishas*. Translated from the French by Emma Craufurd. London: Cassell, 1956.

Yasumatsu, Henry, with Ozawa Shōichi. "Saakasu gei ichidai." In *Sasurau: Saakasu no sekai*, edited by Nagai Hiro'o and Ozawa Shōichi. In *Gei sōsho*, vol. 2, pp. 171–94. Tokyo: Hakusuisha, 1981.

Yōroppa eiga sakuhin zenshū. Tokyo: Kinema junpōsha, 1972.